THE FRENCH REVOLUTION

THE FRENCH REVOLUTION

Conflict or Continuity?

Edited by STEVEN T. ROSS
University of Texas

HOLT, RINEHART AND WINSTON
New York • Chicago • San Francisco • Atlanta
Dallas • Montreal • Toronto • London • Sydney

Cover illustration: The execution of Louis XVI. Dutch
engraving, *ca.* 1800. *(The Granger Collection)*

CONTENTS

Marie Antoinette on the way to the Guillotine. Sketch by Jacques-Louis David. (Bibliothèque Nationale; Roger Jean Segalat)

INTRODUCTION

The dramatic events of the French Revolution still echo in men's imaginations. Even as crowds surged through the streets of Paris, men of letters began denouncing or defending the revolutionaries. Generally the political right opposed the Revolution, moderates accepted certain parts of it, and the left regarded it all, at least until the events of 1794, as the inevitable progression of French history. Each new scholarly generation has brought its own unique insights and techniques to the study of the revolutionary decade, and in the second half of the twentieth century controversy continues to engage historians and students alike.

Traditionally, royalists, conservative and right-wing authors have castigated the Revolution and its leaders. English writer-politician Edmund Burke was among the first to denounce the Revolution which, he asserted, arose from the actions of impractical ideologues who attempted to impose their abstract concept of society upon reality. The incompatibility between the ideal and actual situation led them to become ever more fanatical and violent in their desperate attempt to compel reality to conform to their notions.

In the nineteenth century conservative historians continued to adhere to Burke's outlook. Hippolyte Taine, shaken and horrified by the violence of the 1871 Paris Commune, saw a distinct causal connection between these hostilities and the original revolutionary movement. Taine readily admitted that the old regime had numerous shortcomings but insisted that specific reforms would have been preferable to the enormous disruption caused by efforts to impose an abstract ideological system on the socioeconomic realities of French life. The upheaval of 1789 destroyed an integrated social structure and substituted only a materialistic individualism.

Twentieth-century author Augustin Cochin viewed the Revolution as a conspiracy. The conspiracy theory is old, as old as the Revolution itself. Cochin's contribution is sociological precision. According to him, the Revolution arose from the actions of the intellectuals, a view identical to that of Burke and Taine. Cochin, however, went further and described how the philosopher-radicals operated. Using Masonic lodges, provincial academies, and café reading rooms, this self-styled elite, functioning like an American big-city political machine, spread

1

its propaganda to the ignorant majority and then mobilized them to attack the *status quo*.

Louis Madelin presents an interesting departure from antirevolutionary historiography. While he condemned the Revolution, he also regarded the Bourbon monarchy as weak and ineffectual. As he saw it, Napoleon Bonaparte provided France with internal order and international prestige. Neither the Old Regime nor the Republic governed effectively, and only a strong leader was able to bring the nation tranquility and glory.

In sum, then, antirevolutionary historians have generally condemned the Revolution as un-French and unnecessary, claiming that it arose from no real problems and produced few valuable results. Unrealistic fanatics led the movement; ignorant and uninformed masses followed. Accordingly, the problems besetting modern France can be traced back to the excesses and failures of the eighteenth-century rebellion.

The Revolution also has its legions of defenders. Thomas Paine, a contemporary of Burke, regarded the Revolution as a just and necessary attempt of the French people to assert their rights. François Guizot, a leading figure in the July Monarchy, and his rival Adolphe Thiers, who later became the first president of the Third Republic, both insisted that the Revolution arose from deep-rooted social and economic issues extending far back in the French past. The middle class had been seeking access to political power and social prominence ever since the Middle Ages, and this quest culminated in the Revolution. Both rejected the more radical aspects of the Revolution and denied that these formed an integral part of the revolutionary movement, but they regarded the Revolution as a whole as a beneficial movement because it marked the advent of the bourgeoisie to power.

Republicans and socialists in the nineteenth century also defended the Revolution. Jules Michelet and Alphonse Lamartine, both republicans, defended some of the Revolution's more radical phases. They claimed that the destruction of the monarchy and the creation of the Republic in 1792 were natural consequences of events which began in 1789. They continued to deny, however, that the Reign of Terror and Robespierre's Republic of Virtue were intrinsic parts of the revolutionary movement. Socialist authors, christened by Karl Marx as utopians, did defend Robespierre, claiming that he was gradually moving toward the creation of a system of social justice and equality. The utopians, seeking historical legitimization for themselves, linked Robespierre to Babeuf, a neosocialist who tried unsuccessfully to seize power in 1796, and thence to their own movement. Other socialist writers collected revolutionary journals, pamphlets, and documents, thus making a lasting contribution to revolutionary historiography. Later historians of all political persuasions used these collections.

Although difficult to classify as pro- or antirepublican, Alexis de Tocqueville ranks among the most important historians of the Revolutionary Era. Together with other liberal scholars he believed that the destruction of the Old Regime was the result of certain long-term factors and historical trends, but the causes he described were very different from those of the standard liberal interpretation. Rather than place the blame for the coming of the Revolution on the refusal of governing elites to grant power to the middle class, Tocqueville attributed the collapse of the old order to the crown's misguided policy of centralization. A descendant of a provincial noble family, he argued that the centralization policy deprived France of an English-type service nobility and effective local government. The Bourbons reduced their aristocracy to a parasitic self-seeking pressure group which hindered the central government and antagonized the middle class to the point where it struck out against both the king and the nobles and completed the transformation of France into a centrally administered state. Although further research has cast doubt upon many of Tocqueville's assumptions, his emphasis on the existence of real social divisions within France and his insistence on archival research makes his work of continuing interest to modern scholars.

In the late nineteenth century a close relationship existed between the views of historians of the Revolution and the politics of the Third Republic. Born in the aftermath of the disastrous Franco-Prussian War and the repression of the Paris Commune, the Third Republic enjoyed a tenuous existence at first. Large segments of the French public regarded it as a transitional regime, and for many years its survival was in doubt. By the late 1870s, however, republican parties began to rebuild their strength, and by the 1880s they dominated the political scene. In 1886 the city of Paris established a chair of French revolutionary studies at the Sorbonne. Alphonse Aulard, the first incumbent, was typical of the politically liberal, anticlerical, economically conservative republicans of his time; his scholarship reflected the attitudes of this group.

Aulard saw the Revolution as the product of historical circumstances and argued that revolutionary violence had been necessary to defend the gains of the Revolution against reactionary forces. His special protagonist was Danton. To Aulard, Danton was a democrat and a patriot closely resembling the republicans of the 1880s. Danton fought to protect the Revolution and the soil of France while always seeking peace at home and abroad. If Danton was Aulard's protagonist, Robespierre was his bête noire. Aulard saw Robespierre as a narrow-minded fanatic who drove Danton from power, arranged his judicial murder, and then proceeded to drench the nation in an unnecessary bloodbath in the name of virtue. Aulard also assigned great importance to the conflict between the revolutionaries and the Catholic church, a conflict which still raged in his own time. He believed that one of the Revolution's major triumphs was the weakening of Rome's power and influence in France. Aulard, then, considered the Revolution as primarily a political movement centered around the issues of anticlericalism and democracy.

Historians in the late nineteenth and early twentieth century did not focus their attention exclusively on political questions. Growing numbers began to explore social and economic factors. Influenced by Marxist theory, they brought to their studies a heightened appreciation for the impact of the popular movement and for the work of Robespierre and his followers.

Jean Jaurès, leader of the French socialist party in the years before World War I, was among the first to emphasize the social issue. A Marxist as well as democrat and patriot, Jaurès sought to reconcile the bourgeois revolution of 1789 with modern socialism. He argued that by creating a parliamentary system the revolutionaries had made a peaceful transition to socialism possible. Jaurès also noted the important role played by the Parisian populace and asserted that Robespierre's economic policies were precursors of modern socialism. Jaurès revived and elaborated many of the concepts set forth by his utopian socialist predecessors and attempted to integrate modern Marxism into the Republican tradition.

Like Jaurès, Albert Mathiez emphasized Robespierre's role in the Revolution. Although he was Aulard's student and later his successor at the Sorbonne, Mathiez's view of the Revolution differed from his mentor's on the questions of the importance of the church-state conflict and the social and economic issue. He claimed that Aulard overemphasized the religious problem and neglected the socioeconomic aspects of the Revolution. Disillusioned with the older generation of republican politicians, Mathiez concluded that during the Revolution Danton represented a corrupt and dissolute establishment. In direct contrast to Aulard, Mathiez argued that Danton was a self-serving politican who, despite moderate success, failed to give the nation decisive leadership in time of crisis.

During World War I Mathiez became aware of the importance of government economic regulation, and the Bolshevik Revolution fortified his belief in the importance of the social question and class conflict. These experiences influenced his analysis of Robespierre's policies. According to Mathiez, the period 1793–1794 was one of intense foreign and domestic crisis. France was beset by external war, internal insurrection, and bitter class hostility. Robespierre, representing the democratically minded middle class, made economic concessions to the lower classes in order to win their political support, harness their energies to the national defense effort, and create a more equalitarian society. The Terror, then, was more than a means of securing his faction in power; it was the necessary use of his police power to enforce law and order in a time of grave national crisis.

After 1932 Georges Lefebvre became the leading authority on the Revolution. His interpretation drew heavily on traditional prorevolutionary views bolstered by the insights of Jaurès and Mathiez. Lefebvre, of course, introduced his own unique contributions to revolutionary historiography. He argued that the Revolution was not a single movement but rather a series of parallel revolutions. Several socioeconomic groups, some demanding and others opposing change, pursued their differing objectives, and the interaction of these factions gave the Revolution its shape and substance. When revolutionary groups felt threatened by the forces of counterrevolution, they would unite in what Lefebvre called a defensive reaction and strike out against a real or imagined threat. When the immediate threat subsided, the revolutionary factions would often end their alliance and begin to bicker among themselves. Lefebvre also sought to clarify Robespierre's policies and problems. He stated that Robespierre believed in the ideal of a nation of small independent shopkeepers, artisans, and farmers. The pressures of foreign and civil strife, in addition to the demands of the Parisian populace, forced him to establish a centralized administration and a regulated economy. The pressing need for national discipline led him to strike down opponents on both the left and right. His policies enabled him to lead France successfully through the crisis of 1793–1794, but he failed to win political allies and antagonized many important factions. Consequently, as France began to emerge triumphant, Robespierre was politically isolated and open to attack by his numerous rivals.

Republican historians as a rule tend to regard the Revolution as the culmination of social, political, and economic issues stretching deep into the French past. Circumstance, not conspiracy, is their basic explanation of the Revolution's origins and evolution. Beyond this basic agreement prorevolutionary writers remain deeply divided. Some accept the early stages of the Revolution as a logical outgrowth of French history while rejecting the more radical phases. Others accept some of the radical aspects but refuse to admit that the Terror formed an integral part of the Revolution. Still others assert that Robespierre and the Terror comprise a necessary and logical part of the Revolutionary Era.

Controversy over the causes and nature of the Revolution became interwoven into French political life. Even today an individual's attitude toward the outstanding events and personalities of the Revolution is fairly indicative of his current political orientation. Recent scholarship has, however, tended to turn away from the debate over the causes and nature of the Revolution and has undertaken to conduct detailed examinations of many significant specific aspects of the Revolution. No new synthesis has yet come from this research. Rather, scholars have either clarified traditional assumptions or raised serious questions concerning standard interpretations.

The first section of this book deals with the origins of the Revolution. C. E. Labrousse demonstrates that the economic background of the Revolution does not fit into the traditional poverty or prosperity theories. The Revolution did not occur in an atmosphere of grinding poverty; nor did it originate in a time of thriving prosperity. The Revolution took place against a background of economic growth which had slowed markedly, a situation which was complicated by the government's fiscal problems and a severe agricultural crisis in 1788–1789. Coming after decades of progress, the recession and crisis seemed by comparison all the worse and contributed toward the development of an explosive situation.

Georges Lefebvre, in his famous study of the Revolution, puts forth his concept of parallel revolutions. He also demonstrates how in the initial phases of the Revolution the defensive reaction of the peasants and the urban masses enabled the bourgeoisie to triumph over the forces of counterrevolution.

Other scholars have begun to ask fundamental questions about the nature of the French bourgeoisie. Some have gone so far as to wonder whether a clearly definable middle class, with a common set of class aspirations, existed in 1789. George V. Taylor, for example, argues that the middle class did not consist of business entrepreneurs. Rather, great numbers of successful businessmen sought to emulate the life style of the aristocracy and left commercial enterprise behind as soon as they had amassed sufficient capital to purchase a landed estate and live as country gentlemen. The successful capitalist did not remain in commerce for long either. Rather than reinvest his profits in business ventures, he tended to buy low yield but secure government paper. The middle class was, therefore, far from an integrated socioeconomic pressure group. Taylor's conclusion raises a number of other important questions. Who actually were the revolutionaries of 1789? What were their grievances and objectives? Why did some members of the middle class become revolutionary? Alfred Cobban raises further questions about Lefebvre's interpretations. Cobban asserts that the Revolution was not in fact a major social upheaval and that the business middle class played a negligible role in the events of 1789. He sees the Revolution as a rising of lower-level civil servants, bureaucrats, and lawyers against their entrenched superiors. The work of Taylor and Cobban not only presents a serious challenge to standard views of the Revolution but also points out the need for further detailed study of the French social structure.

The second section deals with popular movements. For some time historians have realized that urban and rural mass movements played a significant role in the Revolution, but only recently have they undertaken a close examination of them. Such research has shown that earlier stereotypes are largely invalid. The city crowds did not consist of criminals, prostitutes, and vagabonds, as conservative commentators would have it; nor were they an aroused proletariat, as the Marxists imply. Similarly, historians must study the structure and characteristics of the French peasantry in order to revise outdated generalizations.

In dealing with urban revolutionary crowds, George Rudé concludes that the typical mob member was an artisan or apprentice, a hard-working, stable individual who, because of the unusual times and circumstances, sought to achieve concrete economic and political objectives through organized force. Albert Soboul agrees with Rudé and goes on to describe the aspirations, organizations, and operations of the Parisian revolutionaries. Finally, Charles Tilly, in dealing with the great counterrevolutionary peasant movement in the Vendée, demonstrates that the Vendean revolt cannot be described in simple terms. It was more that a Catholic revolt against anticlerical republicans, more than a simple outburst of royalism, and more than a provincial rising against Parisian domination. Although much work remains to be done, recent research has deepened historical understanding of the composition and workings of the popular revolutionary movement.

The third section deals with some of the problems surrounding the Terror of 1793–1794. Crane Brinton's pioneering work explores the composition of the Jacobin societies, Robespierre's chief source of political support. Brinton shows that the typical Jacobin was not a power-mad radical, but a stable, prosperous member of upper middle class society. Using sociological techniques, he demonstrates that Jacobin club members formed a good cross section of the politically active well-to-do bourgeoisie. Michael J. Sydenham uses a similar approach to dissect the Jacobin's chief rivals in the republican camp. He argues that the Girondins were not a united party or even a well-organized faction. They were a collection of individuals drawn mainly from the upper bourgeoisie who tried to curb Robespierre's hold on the nation's political life and failed. Robert R. Palmer places Robespierre and the Committee of Public Safety within the crisis framework of 1793. He delineates those factors which led Robespierre and his allies to establish an emergency wartime regime. He also explains the Terror and the violent patriotism of the crisis years as a response of normal men to abnormal circumstances. There remains, however, the perennial question: When does wartime patriotism become fanaticism?

The fourth section presents views of the Directory, the regime that ruled France from 1795 to 1799. Traditionally, historians of all shades of political opinion reviled the Directory as a weak, corrupt, and ineffective institution. Some historians, however, have sought to revise this estimate. Albert Goodwin argues that the Directory was not overly corrupt and was on the whole efficient in domestic affairs. The impact of the French Revolution outside of France and the relationship between revolutionaries in France and foreign radicals has recently attracted scholarly interest. Jacques Godechot maintains that the last decades of the eighteenth century witnessed widespread revolutionary ferment in Europe and the New World. The revolution in France was merely a part of this larger movement, but because of its success France became the focus of the entire process.

The last section reveals some of the issues and problems surrounding the international impact of the Revolution. Franklin L. Ford supplies a general view of the Revolutionary Era and seeks to demonstrate that the period 1789–1815 witnessed fundamental changes in the political, social, and economic structure of European civilization.

Research and debate on the French Revolution has by no means ended. Although historians have reached agreement on many older issues, they continue to apply new techniques, revise standard views, and raise entirely new questions. In the revolutionary twentieth century, scholars and students alike can profitably study the first successful popular revolution of modern times.

In the reprinted selections footnotes appearing in the original sources have in general been omitted unless they contribute to the argument or better understanding of the selection.

C. E. LABROUSSE (b. 1895) has studied the economic background of the Revolution in depth. The selection demonstrates the complexity of the economic situation by means of a detailed study of one aspect of the French economy. Labrousse and his students are currently engaged in further detailed studies of eighteenth-century French economic life.*

C. E. Labrousse

Economic Complexity

Following a long period of market contraction, prices after 1788 once again moved upward. Consumption remained hesitant, but prices nevertheless continued to increase. Government officials in the provinces and the Controller General of Finances at Paris noted this trend, which occurred throughout the kingdom. This vigorous recovery . . . expressed beyond any doubt a general market trend.

The rising prices followed a long period of economic decline; as of 1788 the market experienced prices that it had not known for nine years. The depression seemed over. . . . If the year 1785 marked the lowest price levels, the national price index in the following years rose 63 percent.

This increase must not, however, create a false picture. The recent increase . . . relative to the decline of 1778–1785 (or 1778–1786) does not indicate a corresponding superiority of the upsurge of 1785–1789 (or 1786–1789) to the earlier period of rapidly rising prices:[1] the percentage of decline calculated on the basis of a maximum price level is by nature less than a growth percentage calculated on the basis of a minimum price level. It appears then that according to the national index, prices in 1789 were still 25 percent lower than those of 1778. If the market had indeed moved upward, the time of high prices had not yet returned.

[1] The 1760s and 1770s witnessed rapidly increasing price levels.

*C. E. Labrousse, *La Crise de l'economie française a la fin de l'Ancien Régime et au debut de la Revolution.* (Paris: Presses universitaires de France, 1944), pp. 382–387. Translated by Steven T. Ross.

The effective average variation naturally reveals a more marked change. The variation was quite considerable, attaining, according to the completed national index, 126 percent instead of 63 percent. But here too the prices of 1789 were far from regaining the level of the 1778 maximum and remained more than 25 percent lower, or to be exact 28 percent to 26 percent lower. Thus the previous high price level was not regained . . . but the price level moved up week by week. So rapidly did prices increase that by the end of the year the variation was greatly reduced.

The impact of seasonal price fluctuations was striking. The surge of 1789 was caused for the most part by the high prices of the second half of the year; from Bourgogne to Danphany and from there to the district of Mantauban witnesses agreed that prices rose extremely quickly, but it was in Bourgogne and doubtless in the provinces of the east and northeast that the inflation was most rapid, quickened probably by a decline in production. On the whole the seasonal price fluctuation raised prices in 1789 by 25.3 percent and consequently moved the effective total increase between the average price of 1786 and the seasonal maximum of 1789 from 126 percent to 183 percent. Thus the 1789 maximum remained below the 1778 level even though the former came very close to the latter: the variation between 1789 and 1778 was not more than 13 percent . . . The great superiority of the seasonal variation of 1789 over that of 1778 was the factor which allowed the 1789 price level to gain so much between spring and autumn . . . Thanks to the seasonal variation the price level of 1778 was almost regained by the end of the first revolutionary year.

In the southern wine-growing regions, where the depression was exceptionally severe and prices had fallen accordingly, there was a startling and rapid upswing.

From the low point of 1786 to 1789 prices in the south more than doubled . . . The market of the Midi which had been feeble reacted with much more force than other markets. The price increase of 1787, which was particularly notable in the southern maritime wine trade, seems to arise from an increase in foreign consumption of French wine resulting from the implementation of the Anglo-French Commercial treaty of 1786. It was not caused by a poor harvest. The wine left by sea, and as usual the maritime wine trade was critically important. The superiority of the increase of southern prices, even more marked in the ensuing year, seems to correspond to an increase in demand both foreign and domestic. The impact of the two factors tended to come together in 1789, and prices in the Midi registered a continuous increase. Here the impact of supply and demand does not appear to be without effect. The Midi's harvest was markedly inferior in 1788 to the harvests of the east and northeast and doubtless to all of the other wine-growing regions. At the same time consumers, less harmed by the economic crisis, offered little resistance to the price increase. Another factor however, had a contrary effect. The appearance of the harvest, which had an impact on the market during the course of the year, and if the appearance was an accurate forecast for 1789, the harvest was going to be poor in the Midi and even worse elsewhere. This factor would cause a continental price increase of great violence although the increase would take place too late to influence completely the annual price index. Only at the end of the second half of the year would continental prices rise more drastically than others.

The national fluctuation of prices, dominated by the general contraction of supply and demand but varying slightly from time to time and region to region and by the diversity of demand levels was in general most notable in the Midi when compared to the previous minimum.

It is important to note that prices should be compared to the minimum levels and not to the maximum of 1778. Prices in the Midi had been exceptionally high in 1778; the depression had been severe, and the Midi's prices did not begin to recover until after those of other areas. The continental prices rose most rapidly in 1789, but the national price index in general and the Midi prices in particular remained below the 1778 levels. Nationally, prices in 1789 were 11 percent below those of 1778 while the southern variation was 38 percent below the 1778 level. The substitution of effective price movement for changes in the national index of prices generally confirms these differences in percentages. If, for example, instead of comparing the single years 1778 and 1789 or comparing groups of years such as 1778–1779, years of high prices, with the years of recovery 1787–

1789, the results would remain basically the same.

The intervention of seasonal movements accentuates the difference in prices between the Midi and other areas. Continental prices rose fastest in 1789. The addition of this seasonal movement in the Midi, calculated on the basis of prices in Danphany and Montauban, compared to other districts based on prices in Bourgogne emphasizes the contrast between the two zones. Outside the Midi the price curve reached and passed the price level of 1778, while in the Midi prices remained in 1789 a quarter less than the 1778 level.

Even in 1789 the price depression created during the period 1780–1787 persisted at least partially in the Midi. The rapid recovery in the years following 1787 tended to attenuate it. But prices did not regain all they had lost. Midi prices as well as prices in the great wine-growing regions were by the end of 1789 still far from the prices of the peak years of prosperity.

GEORGES LEFEBVRE (1874–1959), one of the leading historians of the French Revolution, began his scholarly career with an impressive study of the peasantry of northern France. In a wealth of articles, books, and essays he went on to deal with many important aspects of the Revolution. His general history of the Revolution, from which this selection is drawn, has become a standard interpretative treatment of the subject.*

Georges Lefebvre

The Popular Revolution

Resort to arms transformed the struggle of social orders into civil war which, abruptly changing the character of the Revolution, gave it a scope that far surpassed what the bourgeoisie had intended or expected. Popular intervention, which provoked the sudden collapse of the social system of the Old Regime, issued from progressive mobilization of the masses by the simultaneous influences of the economic crisis and the convocation of the Estates-General. These two causes fused to create a mentality of insurrection.

The Economic Crisis

Starting in 1778, the surge in production which had followed the Seven Years War and which is known as the splendour of Louis XV, was checked by difficulties rooted in agricultural fluctuations, a continual problem of the old economy. These setbacks became established in cyclical depressions and caused what their historian[1] called the decline of Louis XVI. First, unusually heavy grape harvests provoked a dreadful slump in the wine market. Prices fell by as much as 50 percent. They rose somewhat after 1781 because of scarcity, but short supply then meant that the wine sector could not recoup its losses. Wine-growing was still practised in almost every part of the kingdom and for many peasants was the most profitable market product. They suffered cruelly; those

---

[1] C. E. Labrousse, whose work appears in this section. — Ed.

---

*Georges Lefebvre, *The French Revolution from Its Origins to 1793*, translated by E. M. Evanson (New York: Columbia University Press, 1962), pp. 116–130. Footnotes omitted.

who were sharecroppers found their income reduced to nothing. Grain prices were the next to fall, remaining relatively low until 1787. Finally, a drought in 1785 killed off much of the livestock.

Rural inhabitants constituted the majority of consumers, and because their purchasing power was reduced industrial production was in turn threatened after 1786. Traditional interpretation has laid primary blame for industry's troubles upon the commercial treaty with Britain [the Eden Treaty of 1786]. Although this was not the most important cause, it certainly did obstruct industry temporarily, since production had to modernize if it was to withstand foreign competition. Unemployment spread. The countryside, where domestic industry had developed, suffered as much as the cities.

The lower classes therefore had no reserves left when they faced the brutal prospect of famine after grain crops failed in 1788. The price of bread rose steadily. At the beginning of July, 1789, a pound of bread sold for four sous in Paris—where the government nevertheless sold its imported grains at a loss—and twice as much in some provinces. At that time wage earners considered two sous per pound the highest price they could possibly pay and still subsist, for bread was their staple food and average daily consumption ranged from one and a half pounds per person to two or three for an adult manual labourer. Necker ordered large purchases from abroad, and, as usual, labour centres [*ateliers de charité* or public workshops] opened up, while measures were taken for distributing soup and rice. The previous winter had been severe, and the cruel effects of high prices did not lessen as the harvest season drew near. For over a half-century we have known, chiefly from the works of Jaurès, that the prosperity of the kingdom of France was responsible for the growing power of the bourgeoisie, and in

this sense it is with reason that [the historian] Michelet's interpretation has been attacked, for the Revolution broke out in a society in the midst of development, not one crippled and seemingly threatened with collapse by nature's Providential shortages. But the social importance of this enrichment should not deceive us. Since colonial profits were realized mainly through re-exportation, the nation's labour force did not benefit as much as we might think, and, while a long-term rise in prices swelled the income of large landowners and bourgeoisie, wages failed to keep pace. We now know that production was dislocated and curtailed in the last decade before the Revolution; and we can justifiably state that the living standard of the masses was steadily declining. Famine, when it came, overwhelmed the populace.

"The people" (artisans, shopkeepers, hired help) as well as proletarians ("the populace"), peasants—small proprietors and sharecroppers who did not raise enough to support themselves or wine growers who did not raise any grain—as well as townsmen unanimously agreed that the government and upper classes were responsible for these afflictions. Income declined but taxes did not. Tolls and duties on consumption became more hateful in times of high prices. If the wine market was restricted it was because excises limited consumption. There was no bread because Brienne removed controls on grain exports and shipments in 1787. True, Necker had stopped exports, subsidized imports, and reinstituted market sales. But he was too late. "Hoarders" had gone to work. Anyone in authority, all government agents were suspected of participating in hoarding. The "famine plot" was thought to be more than a myth. Tithe collectors and lords were just as odious—they were hoarders because their levies cut into a poor harvest and consumed the peasants' supplies. The final blow was that collectors and lords profited even more from the high prices that increased poverty. And, finally, the solidarity of the Third Estate was shaken: the grain merchant, the baker, and the miller were all threatened; the bourgeois, partisan of economic freedom, clashed with popular hostility towards capitalism, since the people by nature favoured requisitions and controls. In April Necker authorized requisitions to replenish the markets, but the intendants and municipal officials rarely used this power.

As the months of 1789 passed, riots kept the tired and frightened officials in a constant state of alert. On April 28 Parisian workers from the faubourg Saint-Antoine sacked the manufactories of Réveillon and Henriot. Throughout the kingdom markets were the scenes of disturbances. Grain shipments, forced by milling and transportation conditions to use roads and rivers in plain view of famished hordes, were sometimes halted. The army and constabulary exhausted themselves rushing from one place to another, but were not inclined to deal harshly towards rebels whose privations they shared and unconsciously began to feel a common sympathy with them. The armour of the Old Regime was rapidly disintegrating.

Agitation was especially pronounced in the countryside. There the tax burden was crushing; tithes and manorial dues drove the peasants to desperation. Sentiment in the peasant community was divided among journeymen, sharecroppers, small proprietors, and large-scale tenant farmers, but on all matters of taxation it was solidly opposed to royal authority and the aristocracy. Tremors of agrarian revolt could be felt well before July 14 — in Provence at the end of March, around Gap in April, in Cambrésis and Picardy in May. Near Versailles and Paris game had been exterminated, forests cleaned out. More-

over, the people were afraid of each other because begging, a regional trouble, spread before their eyes. Many journeymen and small landowners became mendicants. The poor left their villages to crowd into towns or else became vagabonds, forming groups which coursed through the country. They invaded farms even at night, forced themselves in by the fear of burning and of attacks on livestock, trees, the crops that were just beginning to grow, or by threatening to pillage everything. Officials had their own reasons for worrying about the crops and let the villagers arm themselves for protection. As fear of brigandage spread, panics broke out. The slightest incident was enough to put a timid person to flight, convinced that brigands had arrived, sowing fear wherever he fled.

The "Good News" and the Great Hope

But we cannot be sure that economic crisis would have driven the people to aid the bourgeoisie if the calling of the Estates-General had not deeply moved the populace. The goals appropriated by the bourgeois they elected scarcely concerned the lower classes, but an event so foreign was welcomed as "a good piece of news" presaging a miraculous change in men's fates. It awoke hopes both dazzling and vague of a future when all would enjoy a better life — hopes shared by the bourgeoisie. This vision of the future united the heterogeneous elements of the Third Estate and became a dynamic source of revolutionary idealism. Among the common people it gave to the Revolution a character that can be called mythical, if myth is taken to mean a complex of ideas concerning the future which generate energy and initiative. In this sense the Revolution in its early stages can be compared to certain religious movements in nascent form, when the poor gladly discern a return to paradise on earth.

Arthur Young [the British traveller and agricultural reformer] has recorded that on July 12, while walking up a hill near Les Islettes, in the Argonne Forest, he met a poor woman who described her misery to him. "'Something was to be done by some great folk for such poor ones,' but she did not know who nor how, 'but God send us better, *car les tailles et les droits nous écrasent*'" (for the *taille* and [*manorial*] rights are crushing us).

Since the king consulted his people, he pitied their plight. What could he do if not remove their burdens—taxes, tithes, fees? He would therefore be content if they went ahead and helped him: after the elections aristocratic cries of alarm arose on all sides, for the peasants openly declared that they would pay no more.

At the same time this great hope inflamed fearful passions, from which the bourgeoisie was not exempt. The revolutionary mentality was imbued with them; the history of the period bears their deep imprint.

The Aristocratic Conspiracy and the Revolutionary Mentality

The Third Estate was at once convinced that the nobles would stubbornly defend their privileges. This expectation, soon confirmed by aristocratic opposition to the doubling and then to the vote by head, aroused suspicions that with little difficulty hardened into convictions. The nobles would use any means to "crush" the villagers; they would outwit their well-intentioned king to obtain dissolution of the Estates-General. They would take up arms, bar themselves in their châteaux, and enlist brigands to wage civil war just as the king's agents enlisted

the poverty-stricken. Prisoners would be released and recruited. Nobles who had already hoarded grain to starve the Third Estate would willingly see the harvest ruined. Fear of the aristocracy was everywhere rapidly linked with fear of brigands, a connection that fused the results of the calling of the Estates with those of the economic crisis. Moreover, foreign powers would be called on to help. The comte d'Artois was going to emigrate and win over his father-in-law (the king of Sardinia), the Spanish and Neapolitan Bourbons, and the emperor, brother of the queen. France, like Holland, would be invaded by the Prussians. Collusion with foreign powers, which weighed heavily in the history of the Revolution, was assumed from the beginning, and in July an invasion was feared imminently. The whole Third Estate believed in an "aristocratic conspiracy."

The burden of royal centralization and the conflict of orders dominated the Third Estate's view of the crisis. Neglecting to accuse natural forces and incapable of analysing the total economic situation, the Third laid responsibility upon royal power and the aristocracy. An incomplete picture perhaps, but not inexact. The freeing of the grain trade, which Brienne had decreed, did favour speculators; to the argument that this would increase production the people replied that it would profit the aristocracy and bourgeoisie first, while they had to bear the costs. Similarly, if the Third Estate falsely imputed Machiavellian qualities to the aristocracy, it was true that the court, in agreement with the nobles, thought to punish the deputies for their insubordination; and it was true that the aristocratic conspiracy, although denounced prematurely, was soon to become a reality. In any case the mind of the Third Estate is of capital interest in showing the historian that events have their immediate roots not in their antecedents but in the men who intervene by interpreting those events.

If aristocratic conspiracy and "brigands" instilled many with enough fear to cause occasional panics, there were others who, although frightened, remained rational and faced danger resolutely. Consequently the labels "fears" and "Great Fear" unjustly imply that the whole Third Estate was struck dumb with terror. Actually the revolutionary mentality was capable of countering unrest with vigorous defensive reaction. The Third was kept informed by letters from its deputies and in turn encouraged its representatives with innumerable appeals. The bourgeoisie would gladly have pushed further: it wanted to take municipal control from the petty oligarchy made up of those who owned offices, many of whom had acquired noble titles. At Paris the electors who had chosen deputies organized a secret municipal council in the Hôtel de Ville at the end of June. Notables hoped to set up a "national militia" [soon to be called the National Guard]. This was proposed by Parisian electors to the Constituent Assembly, but deputies did not dare authorize it. A double purpose lay behind the desire to organize a militia: to resist royal troops should the occasion rise, and to hold the people in check. Meanwhile efforts were made to win over the army, not without success, since lower-ranking officers had no hope of advancement and the soldiers, who had to pay for part of their subsistence, were affected by high prices. The French Guards fraternized with crowds at the Palais Royal; at the end of June the people freed prisoners at the Abbaye. Several men are known to have distributed money among the soldiers or to have paid the July in-

surgents. Beyond doubt the agents of the duc d'Orléans did as much.

Finally, along with the defensive reaction there existed a punitive will either to cripple the aristocratic conspiracy, hoarders, and all enemies of the people, or to punish those enemies. From July on this took the form of imprisonments, acts of brutality, and popular massacres.

These three aspects of the revolutionary mentality—fear, defensive reaction, and punitive will—together constitute one of the keys to the unfolding narrative of the French Revolution. The conspiracy was to all appearances halted by the end of 1789, and repression slackened. The plot later reappeared, cloaked with many of the characteristics given it in advance, and foreign powers came to its aid. The resulting defensive reaction first stimulated the volunteers who poured in and then was responsible for the mass levy. Punitive will provoked the massacres of 1792 and, when danger again loomed in 1793, the Convention warded off further perils only by setting up the Terror. Fear and its accompaniments died out only, and gradually, after the uncontested triumph of the Revolution.

The Parisian Revolution

Against this background, Necker's dismissal was a torch set to a powder keg: it was taken as evidence that the aristocratic conspiracy had begun to act. News of the event circulated in Paris on Sunday, July 12. The weather was good and a crowd gathered at the Palais Royal, whose garden and arcades, recently opened by the duc d'Orléans, had become a centre of amusement. Groups clustered about extemporaneous orators; only one, Camille Desmoulins, do we know by name. Soon processions of demonstrators reached the boulevards, then the Rue Saint-Honoré. The cavalry undertook to make them disperse and charged the crowd at the Place Louis XV. The French Guards in return attacked the cavalry. The baron de Besenval, military commander, mustered his whole following on the Champ de Mars that evening.

The Parisians did not think of rallying to the aid of the Assembly; they saved it, but only indirectly. They were concerned with their own fate, convinced that their city, surrounded by royal troops and brigands, would first be bombarded from Montmartre and the Bastille and then would be pillaged. Panics erupted continually during these "days," Act One of the Great Fear. The police were gone. Toll gates were burned. [The monastery of] Saint-Lazare was sacked. Person and property were seemingly endangered. Fright hovered over the capital, abandoned to its own resources.

A defensive reaction followed immediately. Barricades arose in the streets, and gunsmiths' stores were wiped clean. The electors appointed a permanent committee and set up a militia. To arm their forces, they took 32,000 guns from the Invalides on the morning of July 14. In search of more, they went to the Bastille. Its governor, de Launay, parleyed. Commanding only a small garrison, he had ordered the outer courts evacuated. They were quickly filled by the crowd. Behind walls ninety feet high, surrounded by a water-filled ditch seventy-five feet wide, he had no cause to fear an attack. But he lost his nerve and opened fire. Several men fell; others drew back in disorder, crying treason, convinced that they had been permitted to advance only to offer better aim. Shots rang out from those who were armed, and battle was engaged, but on an entirely unequal basis: the assailants lost

a hundred men, whereas one sole member of the garrison was hit. A census was later taken among the "conquerors of the Bastille," so we know a good number of the attackers. All classes of society were represented among them, but most were artisans from the faubourg Saint-Antoine.

The tide of battle was still uncertain when the French and National Guards arrived from the Hôtel de Ville. Led by a former non-commissioned officer named Hulin and by Lieutenant Élie, they entered the courtyard of the Bastille and under heavy fire aimed their cannons at the gate. De Launay took fright and offered to give himself up. Élie accepted, but the attackers protested—No surrender! Amid total confusion the governor had the drawbridge lowered, and the crowd rushed across into the fortress. Efforts to save most of the defenders were successful, but three officers and three men were massacred. De Launay was with difficulty led to the doors of the Hôtel de Ville, where he lost his life. Shortly after, Flesselles, provost of the merchants [the title of the chief municipal official of Paris], was also killed. Their heads were paraded through the city on pikes.

Besenval ordered a retreat to Saint-Cloud. The electors took over municipal control, appointed Bailly mayor, and offered command of the National Guard to Lafayette, who soon afterwards gave the Guard a cockade of red and blue, the colours of Paris, between which he placed a white band, the king's colour. Through Lafayette the tricoloured flag, emblem of the Revolution, joined old France with the new.

No one considered the Bastille the stakes of the struggle, and at first no one thought that its fall would determine the outcome. Panics continued. But seizure of the Bastille, of mediocre importance in itself, broke the court's resistance.

The forces Versailles had on hand were not enough to take Paris, especially since the loyalty of the troops was not certain. Louis hesitated. Would he try to flee? Against the urgings of the comte d'Artois he decided to give in. On July 15 he yielded to the Assembly and announced the dismissal of his troops. The next day he recalled Necker. On the 17th he went to Paris and accepted the cockade.

Few concluded from this that the aristocracy had laid down its arms, and wild rumours continued to circulate. The comte d'Artois and many other emigrated; according to one story an English squadron lay in wait off the coast of Brest. The permanent committee searched the edges of Paris for brigands. Finding only vagabonds, it sent them back where they had come from. The suburbs feared that they would be overrun with such wanderers, and panic spread. Bertier de Sauvigny, the intendant of Paris, his father-in-law, Foullon de Doué, and Besenval himself were arrested. Massacres began again: on July 22 Sauvigny and Doué were hanged at the Place de Grève; Necker returned just in time to save Besenval on July 30. These murders provoked strong protest, but now part of the bourgeoisie, roused by the obvious danger, joined the people in their fury—"Is this blood then so pure?" cried Barnave before the Constituent Assembly. Nevertheless, they could hardly deny that summary executions ought to cease. On July 23 a notary from the Rue de Richelieu proposed, in the name of his district, that a popular tribunal be set up; and on the 30th Bailly made a similar request. The Assembly paid no heed. Only in October did it institute prosecution for crimes of *lèse-nation* [treason against the people], to be handled by the Châtelet of Paris—an ordinary court. In July the Assembly did at least establish a "committee of investigation," . . . ; and the municipality of Paris organized another which was the first revolutionary committee. While debating the issue of privacy of correspondence during the summer, deputies of all representation, from the marquis de Gouy d'Arsy and Target, member of the Académie Française, to Barnave and Robespierre, firmly maintained that one could not govern in time of war and revolution as in time of peace—in other words, that the rights they were proposing to grant to all citizens depended upon circumstances. This was to become the doctrine of the revolutionary government.

The Municipal Revolution

In the provinces, too, Necker's dismissal provoked strong feeling and an immediate reaction. The populace was no longer content only to send addresses, now often menacing, to its representatives. In several towns the public coffers were broken open and arsenals or military storehouses looted. One committee undertook to set up a militia and issued an appeal to neighbouring communes, even to the peasants. The governor of Dijon was arrested; nobles and priests were confined to their dwellings—this was the first example of detention of suspects. At Rennes the townsmen persuaded the garrison to desert and then rose up. The military commander fled.

When news came of the fall of the Bastille and of the king's visit to Paris —an event celebrated in some places— the bourgeoisie took heart and laid hands on the instruments of control in almost every area. The "municipal revolution," as it is known, was in most cases a peaceable one: the municipal councils of the Old Regime took on notables or stepped down for the electors. Very often they had to create, or permit the formation of, a permanent committee. It was charged initially with organization of the National Guard, but gradually absorbed the whole administrative apparatus. Nevertheless, the people, having taken part in bourgeois demonstrations, demanded that bread prices be lowered. If this was not soon granted riots broke out, the houses of officials and those known as hoarders were sacked, and often the former municipal councils were ousted.

The municipal revolution thus differed from place to place and was often arrested half way. In every instance, however, the only orders obeyed were those of the National Assembly. The king no longer commanded authority. Centralization, too, was weakened: each municipality wielded absolute power within its own confines and over surrounding districts as well. From August on, towns started to conclude mutual-assistance pacts, spontaneously transforming France into a federation of communes. Local autonomy opened the field of action to a small group of resolute men who, without waiting for instructions from Paris, passed what measures they considered necessary to secure public safety. This was a basic stimulant to revolutionary defence.

Yet the other side of the coin was immediately visible. The Constituent Assembly enjoyed a prestige accorded none of its successors, but the populace observed only such decrees as suited it. What did the people want above all else? Tax reform, abolition of indirect levies, institution of controls over the grain trade. Tax collection was suspended; the salt tax, excises, and municipal tolls were suppressed; exchange of grains was either forbidden or continually thwarted. Proclamations and decrees against this

had no effect. At Paris the populace went even further. Within the districts — divisions established for elections to the Estates-General — assembled citizens, like the electors before them, claimed to supervise the municipal authority they set up to replace the electors. In their eyes national sovereignty entailed direct democracy, an idea that would remain dear to the sans-culottes.

The Peasant Revolution and the Great Fear

The countryside had joined the towns, but revolution in Paris had even greater effect on rural areas. Agrarian revolt broke out in several regions. In the woodlands of Normandy, in the Hainaut and Upper Alsace, châteaux or abbeys were attacked by those seeking to burn archives and force surrender of manorial rights. In Franche-Comté and the Mâconnais peasants set fire to many châteaux, sometimes laying them waste. The bourgeoisie was not always spared: they, too, had to pay. In Alsace the Jews suffered. On the other hand, there was clear evidence of rural hostility towards a menacing capitalism whose instrument had become the manorial reaction: free pasturage was reclaimed, enclosures destroyed, forests invaded, commons taken back or demanded for the first time — the peasant revolution was a double-edged sword. Faced with this threat, the notables drew closer together. Urban militias were used to restore order. In the Mâconnais the bourgeoisie set up extraordinary tribunals beside the old provost courts, and thirty-three peasants were hanged. Revolt fired men's minds. Even more important, however, was a passive resistance which everywhere interfered with collection of the tithe or the *champart*[2] demanded from crops harvested. Only those who wished to pay did so. The Great Fear gave irresistible force to this movement.

Events in Paris strengthened fear of the aristocratic conspiracy, of foreign invasion which could carry it out, of recruitment of brigands for its service. Brigands were the source of even greater fear now that the wheat was ripe, and Paris, along with other large towns, was expelling beggars and vagabonds. Grain riots and agrarian revolts heightened tension. So did forays by National Guards who left towns to pillage châteaux or demand grain. The Great Fear grew out of six localized incidents no different from those which had unloosed so many panics, but this time they set off currents which were fed along the way by new outbreaks acting as relay reinforcements. Some of these can be traced for hundreds of miles, with branches that covered entire provinces. This extraordinary diffusion in a chain reaction gives the Great Fear its distinctive character and illuminates the mentality that made it possible.

A "disturbance" at Nantes alarmed Poitou. At Estrées-Saint-Denis, in the Beauvais, another spread fright in all directions. A third in southern Champagne sowed terror through the Gâtinais, Bourbonnais, and Burgundy. A fourth, originating near the Montmirail forest, close to La Ferté-Bernard, alerted Maine, Normandy, Anjou, and the Touraine. From the edge of the Chizé forest fear struck Angoulême, spread into Berry and the central mountains, alarmed Aquitaine as far as the Pyrenees. In the east, agrarian revolts in Franche-Comté and the Mâconnais drove fear to the shores of the Mediterranean.

---

[2] [A manorial rent payable in kind.]

Revolutionaries and aristocrats accused one another of having contrived the Great Fear. The enemies of the Revolution, charged the revolutionaries, sowed anarchy in an effort to paralyse the National Assembly. The bourgeoisie, replied the aristocrats, alarmed the people to make them take up arms and rebel just when the lower classes desired to remain at peace. This last version met with success because the Great Fear provoked a defensive reaction which turned upon the aristocracy. Near Le Mans and in Vivarais three nobles were put to death, and peasants in the Dauphiné provided a formidable relay station for panic by burning châteaux.

It was therefore repeated afterwards that fear had broken out everywhere and at once, spread by mysterious messengers and engendering agrarian revolt. It did not, in fact, cover the whole kingdom: Brittany, Lorraine, lower Languedoc, among other areas, were unaffected. The Great Fear lasted from July 20 to August 6. Documents show that some propagated it in good faith, and one significant fact is that it never touched the districts which had previously witnessed insurrection. Only in Dauphiné did it provoke a *jacquerie* [large-scale peasant revolt]. If it encouraged the revolution of the peasants it did not cause it. They were already on their feet.

The Night of August 4 and the Declaration of the Rights of Man and the Citizen

While popular revolution spread, the Assembly's debates dragged on ineffectively. Was this the appropriate moment to publish a declaration of rights? Would it not be better to postpone any such action until the constitution was drawn up, so that the two could be reconciled? Arguments of a general nature were voiced with no mention of the reasons behind opposing views: the existence of orders and the privileges, both of which would be suppressed by the principles to be proclaimed. Aristocrats therefore favoured postponement, hoping to preserve a few of their prerogatives, while the Patriots, growing impatient, accused the nobles of undue obstruction, and the more clairvoyant suspected that privileges held by provinces and towns gave the nobility secret supporters within the Third Estate. On the morning of August 4 the Assembly ruled that it would begin by voting the declaration. But its members could expect discussion to provoke new resistance.

On the other hand, the popular revolution had to be resolved. The Assembly, which it had saved, had no choice but to endorse it, yet order had to be re-established, since the people were quietly waiting for the reforms their representatives would deem appropriate. The bourgeoisie in all probability could control townsmen, but the peasants were a different matter. They were destroying the manorial regime without concerning themselves about the Assembly. What course should be taken? If it resorted to the army and provost courts, the Assembly would break with the people and place itself at the mercy of king and aristocracy. The alternative was to grant satisfaction to the rebels—but then how would the parish priests and liberal nobles react? And it was their support which had assured the Third Estate's victory.

The terms of the decision and the tactics to carry it out were decreed during the night of August 3–4 by a hundred deputies meeting at the Café Amaury as a "Breton Club," which dated back to the end of April, when deputies from Brittanny had, as soon as they arrived in town, adopted the custom of concerting their moves and had immediately opened their debates to colleagues from other provinces. They resolved to sway the Assembly by "a kind of magic." In matters involving the feudal system, the duc d'Aiguillon was to take the lead.

But on the evening of August 4 it was the vicomte de Noailles who made the first move, and there was no alternative but to support him. Without debate the Assembly enthusiastically adopted equality of taxation and redemption of all manorial rights except for those involving personal servitude—which were to be abolished without indemnification. Other proposals followed with the same success: equality of legal punishment, admission of all to public office, abolition of venality in office, conversion of the tithe into payments subject to redemption, freedom of worship, prohibition of plural holding of benefices, suppression of annates (the year's income owed the pope by a bishop upon investiture). Privileges of provinces and towns were offered as a last sacrifice. Nevertheless, the "magic" had worked its powers.

These resolutions had to be written up formally, so the debate opened again the next day and lasted until August 11. The final decree began: "The National Assembly destroys the feudal regime in its entirety." This was far from exact: they retained the law of primogeniture and honorific prerogatives, while requirement of an indemnity promised a long life to manorial fees. The tithe was suppressed without indemnity, but, just as fees could be collected until the method of redemption was determined, the tithe could be exacted until a law on public worship was passed.

Despite these qualifications, on the night of August 4 the Assembly achieved in principal the legal unity of the nation. It destroyed the feudal system and aristocratic domination over rural areas; it launched fiscal and ecclesiastical reform. The way was paved for discussion of a declaration of rights. This started on August 20 and continued without intermission until the 26th. Proclaiming liberty, equality, and national sovereignty, the text was in effect the "act of decease" of the Old Regime, which had been put to death by the popular revolution.

GEORGE V. TAYLOR (b. 1919), of the University of North Carolina, has studied the structure of French capitalism in the last decades of the eighteenth century. The following selection from one of his articles challenges some of the traditional views concerning the composition and attitudes of the French bourgeoisie.*

George V. Taylor

Was There a Capitalistic Middle Class?

To call the French Revolution of 1789 a "bourgeois revolution" invokes ideas which, by common consent, are inseparable from that phrase. It implies, for example, a social class created and nurtured by capitalism, with its wealth preponderantly capitalist in form and function and its values largely derived from capitalism. It implies that the relation of this class to the processes of production differed substantially from that of other classes and that, allowing for a reasonable number of eccentricities, the bourgeoisie showed an over-all unity of goals and outlook, related significantly to capitalism, that made its political action meaningful, powerful, and revolutionary. Stripped of these associations, the phrase "bourgeois revolution" (or "revolutionary bourgeoisie") loses most of its interpretive value, including particularly its involvement with a concept of economic change and class struggle ranging from the Middle Ages to the cold war and beyond.

The ideas that comprise this interpretation have now come under criticism, chiefly from Alfred Cobban. . . . Cobban argues that the concepts embodied in the words "bourgeois revolution" disagree with what research has brought to light. He believes that the phrase incorporates a self-confirming system of deception. Taken in its ordinary sense, it acts as a standard for selecting, interpreting, and arranging evidence, and because of this

---

*George V. Taylor, "Noncapitalist Wealth and the Origins of the French Revolution," in *American Historical Review*, LXXII, no. 2 (1967), pp. 469–491. Footnotes omitted.

the research usually ends by confirming assumptions that creep in with the terminology. . . . As a corrective, he calls for a reform of the vocabulary, challenging, among other things, the equivalence of "bourgeois" to "capitalist," and of "noble" to "feudal," and there are others who share his dissatisfaction. I have myself found that there were under the old regime not one kind of capitalism but three, that in comparison with nineteenth-century capitalism they were relatively primitive, and that nobles held a heavy stake in two of them. . . .

All this suggests that what has long seemed a settled explanation of the French Revolution has become the source of growing dissatisfaction and is up for a reappraisal. . . . This reappraisal is far from complete. The range of topics involved in a full examination of the bourgeois revolution model is very broad; the issues are economic, social, political, and even intellectual. . . . But the fundamental question is certainly whether the bourgeoisie of 1789, however defined, had any economic consistency that opposed it to other classes grounded in different forms of wealth. This paper has to do with distinctions between capitalist and noncapitalist wealth and what these imply about the revolution of the upper Third Estate, the movement that began with the demand for doubling the representation of the Third Estate and voting by head rather than by order. It also offers a way of explaining that revolution without having recourse to the present terminology.

There was in the economy of the old regime a distinct configuration of wealth, noncapitalist in function, that may be called "proprietary." It embodied investments in land, urban property, venal office, and annuities. The returns it yielded were modest, ranging between 1 and 5 per cent, but they were fairly constant and varied little from year to year. They were realized not be entrepreneurial effort, which was degrading, but by mere ownership and the passage of calendar intervals. Risk was negligible. Although bad harvests lowered rents in kind, they never destroyed capital, and the rents in money, like annuities and salaries of venal office, were payable regardless of natural hazards. In the proprietary sector investments were almost fully secure.

Historically and functionally, proprietary wealth was aristocratic. Under the old regime, gentility required a stable fortune that left one free to live with ease and dignity on his revenues. In the fortunes of the Toulouse nobles . . . and of the magistrates of the Paris Parlement . . . it was precisely land, urban property, venal office, and annuities that furnished the income on which these families maintained their way of life. Two considerations discouraged nobles from investing in commerce. First, the social values of aristocracy included a notorious aversion to business as practiced by merchants, merchant manufacturers, and bankers. To invest in "trade" was to risk losing status. The only industries that nobles felt entirely free to develop were those rooted in the land and its resources and growing out of certain exploitations of the medieval fief—mines, metallurgy, paper, glass, and canals—and in developing these they adopted practices and forms of organization substantially different from those employed by the merchants. Second, the risks inherent in business endangered the solidity and continuity considered essential to wealth meant to support a family for several generations. Fundamentally, the fortune that best served the interests of an aristocratic family was an endowment. Like an endowment, it was carefully managed, and risk was kept to a minimum. The preference for this kind of wealth, based on ingrained social attitudes that have powerfully retarded French economic growth, survived the Revolution. . . . Both before and after the Revolution, the social values of the old elite dominated the status-conscious men and women of the wealthy Third Estate. Avid for standing, they had little choice but to pursue it as the aristocracy defined it, and the result was a massive prejudice that diverted *roturier* as well as noble wealth into comparatively sterile proprietary investments.

In describing this system of wealth, the word "proprietary" does better than "feudal." . . . The seigneury, consisting of dues, monopolies, and rights surviving from the fief, was an order of property superimposed on property in fee simple, and it could be and was acquired by nonnobles. But seigneurial rights figured marginally in a larger preference for all long-term assets yielding secure revenues and standing, a taste for "property" in every form, not only seigneuries but domains, farms, *métairies*,[1] meadows, fields, stands of timber, forges and mills that could be rented out, houses, buildings, venal offices, and loans of indefinite duration producing annuities called *rentes perpétuelles.* Such properties were enduring. Combined into endowments yielding assured revenues, carefully managed, they could be made to support a family indefinitely in a genteel style of living. . . . The term "proprietary" described these fortunes not only

because it is derived from "property" but also because it echoes the old regime term *propriétaire,* a prestige counter claimed by those who owned land, even in trifling amounts.

The fondness for land penetrated all levels of French society. Profoundly rural, most eighteenth-century Frenchmen had an atavistic attachment to the soil, and "living nobly" was habitually identified with at least seasonal residence in the country. The aristocracy by tradition and the wealthy urban groups by emulation showed an incurable esteem for rural property. . . . People bought land yielding 1 or 2 per cent with funds that could have been deposited with merchants at 5, and borrowed at 5 to buy land that yielded 1 or 2. This passion for land was by no means limited to Grenoble. Nobles, *avocats, procureurs,* financiers, officials, and merchants in all parts of France bought and held urban and rural properties that qualified them for local acceptance, advancement, and privileges. There were shopkeepers, artisans, and even peasants who invested in land and *rentes* that gave them small incomes for old age. In every town those without a business or profession who lived on such investments were taxed on a separate roll, that of the bourgeois, and in 1789 in most towns they voted as a separate electoral group of the Third Estate. A study by Vovelle and Roche shows that the qualification bourgeois disappeared during the Revolution from official acts, and that persons listed under the old regime as bourgeois reappeared in documents of the Directory and the Consulate as *rentiers* and *propriétaires,* demonstrating as well as anything can that before the Revolution the fiscal group called bourgeois was noncapitalist.

Nearly all wealthy landowners exploited their land indirectly, through

---

[1] Land worked by tenant farmers. The lord or owner supplied seed and tools and generally received about 50 percent of the proceeds. — Ed.

tenants. They saw their properties not as profit-making enterprises but as sources of rental income. Rent, in fact, was at the center of all calculations. It was what determined the value of a property: as rent increased, the value grew proportionately, so that, curiously enough, the rate of return on capital remained about the same. Generally speaking, rental income seems to have ranged between 2 and 4 per cent of capital value, and Necker wrote in 1784 that the net revenue from land was 2½ per cent, which is to say that, as an investment, land provided the low but assured return typical of proprietary wealth. When an eighteenth-century proprietor set out to increase the revenue of his properties he thought not in terms of increasing the productivity of the soil but of raising the rent, and in the late eighteenth century a significant rise of the peasant population made this easy to do. As land hunger grew and candidates for leases multiplied, rents rose handsomely. Labrousse has found that, from the base period 1726–1741 to the "intercyclic" period 1785–1789, rural money rents advanced by 98 percent. . . . Where the rent was paid in kind, . . . the rise in rents is difficult to measure, but there is no doubt that it took place. . . . It is perhaps possible to say that the French landowner of the old regime was an exploiter of persons rather than of the soil. The circumstances of the prerevolutionary period did nothing to change his traditional attitudes. Indeed, by enabling him to raise his income without raising production they reinforced them. . . .

In the proprietary scale of preference, the passion for property in office was nearly as strong as that for property in land. A venal office was a long-term investment. Usually it brought a low but stable return, and, as long as the

owner regularly paid the *droit annuel* (in earlier times the *paulette*),[2] he could under restrictions applicable to each office, sell it to a buyer, bequeath it to an heir, or even rent it out to someone. . . . The number and variety of venal offices that existed at the end of the old regime is incredible. An investigation that Necker launched in 1778 disclosed no less than 51,000 venal offices in the law courts, the municipalities, and the financial system, and their capital value, as revealed by voluntary declarations made under an edict of 1771, totaled 600,000,000 livres, although this should be increased by as much as 50 per cent because the declarations, taxable at 1 per cent per annum, were notoriously undervalued. These offices included those held by the personnel of the parlements and their chancelleries, the judges of the other royal courts, and the multitude of clerks, beadles, sergeants, surveyors, assessors, and concessionaires that surrounded these courts. They also included the offices held by the notaries and *procureurs,* who could practice their professions only by acquiring the appropriate *charges.* They did not, however, include the offices of the royal household, venal military appointments, or places in the financial companies and the higher financial concessions like those of the *receveurs généraux des finances,*[3] and for these we should probably add another 200,000,000 or 300,000,000 livres to the total indicated above. Also excluded from these figures were the offices held by guild officials, inspectors, and masters, and particularly by the wigmakers. Given the present state of research we have no

---

[2] An annual tax on the income derived from the post. — Ed.

[3] Many taxes in France were collected by private groups of businessmen who paid the government a fixed sum for them. — Ed.

precise idea of how many adult males owned offices, but it would not be surprising to find that they came to 2 or 3 per cent of the total.

Ordinarily, the declared value of an office was only part of the cost of buying and exercising it. Nearly always, it was sold for a price higher than that recorded in the declarations and contracts, and the investment was increased by heavy taxes, fees for registration and reception, and the honoraria, gratuities, and *pourboires*[4] that a candidate had to distribute to officials, clerks, beadles, and even doormen in obtaining his nomination. . . . When an office gave admission to a profession, the disproportion between its acknowledged value and the full investment was apt to be still greater. . . . In short, the additional costs and professional outlays that accompanied investments in venal office raised the total French private funds committed to this purpose far above the more than 600,000,000 livres with which the Revolution compensated those whose offices it abolished.

Few venal offices were genuinely lucrative. On the 51,000 judicial, municipal, and financial offices covered by the 1778 investigation, the salaries. . . . averaged only 1 per cent of the values declared in 1771, although in most cases there were fees, perquisites, and gratuities that made up the interest on the declared capital. . . . Generally speaking, an investment in office was an investment in standing. What made it desirable was the status, the respectability that it conferred. For a solid gain in prestige, the holders of *charges* would usually settle for a low return and even a loss of capital. . . . In effect, they sacrificed capital for status, which was not unnatural in a society afflicted with a mania for prestige. . . . To the *roturiers* it meant still more to acquire an office that gave noble rank. According to Necker, there were more than four thousand of these, although perhaps half of them, like the magistracies of the parlements, were inaccessible to commoners. For example, a *secrétaire du roi* was ennobled by his office and, if he held it twenty years or died possessed of it, acquired *noblesse transmissible* for his heirs and descendants. A *trésorier de France* enjoyed *noblesse personnelle;* although his family did not share this, there was nothing to prevent him from bequeathing his office to his eldest son, and it appears that some of these offices gave *noblesse transmissible.*[5] According to Necker, there were 900 *secrétaires du roi* attached to the chancelleries of the parlements and 740 places that one takes to be those of the *trésoriers de France* in the financial apparatus. Nothing indicates that the propensity of these offices for creating new nobles had been cut off at the end of the old regime.

In addition to land, urban properties, and office, proprietary wealth was invested in *rentes*. In the broadest sense, a *rente* was an annual revenue that one received for having transferred something of value to someone else. A *rente foncière* was rent for land. A *rente hypothécaire* was an annuity the payment of which was secured by property. A *rente perpétuelle* was an annuity of indefinite duration, terminated only when the debtor chose, on his own initiative, to refund the principal and thereby free himself from paying the *rente*. A *rente viagère* was a life annuity: the principal was entrusted to someone who paid the annuity until the person

---

[4] Tip or bribe.—Ed.

[5] Hereditary or transmissible title.—Ed.

or persons named in the contract died; at that point the principal became finally and irrevocably his. Because the *rente viagère* was essentially a speculation that destroyed all or part of the capital accumulated for a family endowment, most of those living on proprietary wealth believed it reckless and immoral, and a man who converted his fortune into life annuities was considered to have defrauded his heirs.

To an American student, the rationale of this vocabulary is elusive. Everything is clarified, however, by the fact that the vocabulary took shape during the late Middle Ages, when those who wished to borrow, and those who wished to lend, had to find ways of disguising loans at interest so as to circumvent the laws against usury. The terminology of the *rente* made this possible, at least during the sixteenth and seventeenth centuries. One spoke, for example, of purchasing a *rente:* this modulated the smell of avarice and exploitation by making it seem that the lender, who bought the *rente,* had solicited it from the borrower, who sold it, and obtained it on the borrower's terms. The vocabulary also improved appearances by assimilating all these transactions to land rents, which were undoubtedly on the right side of the law. . . .

* * *

It should now be clear that there was a fairly consistent pattern of noncapitalist wealth, that it was traditionally aristocratic, and that "feudalism" is a bad name for it. It was governed by institutional survivals and social values that opposed the progressive and expansive tendencies of capitalism, preferring rent to profit, security to risk, tradition to innovation, and, in terms of personal goals, gentility

to entrepreneurial skill and renown. It displayed nearly all the traits of . . . a traditional society, one dominated by landowners and their values and governed, as far as production was concerned, by pre-Newtonian modes of thought. . . . In England, no doubt, such deterrents to growth existed, but in ways that are not yet clearly explained they were being outflanked or overcome. In France, however, they flourished. The question of why there should have been such a disparity deserves much more study than it has received.

Compared with proprietary wealth, eighteenth-century commercial capitalism seems a vastly different thing. In commerce, banking, and domestic industry fixed assets were negligible, and investments were put into circulating wealth. . . .

Risk, nearly unknown in the proprietary sector, was a central fact of business life. The merchant speculated in commodities, paper, and credit, and, no matter how prudent he was, his fate depended largely on events he could not control. Shipwrecks, acts of war, sudden changes in style, unforeseeable bankruptcies, or unfavorable shifts in exchange rates could wipe him out, and if it was bad luck that broke him it was largely good luck that made him rich. Established merchants, known for caution and probity, went under, while new men, starting with borrowed money and the savings of a clerk's salary, became well to do. Commerce, therefore, was a zone of fortune building and social mobility. But because it lacked the stability of the proprietary sector, it was dangerous for established wealth. . . .

Finally, in contrast to proprietary wealth, business capital gave low dividends in prestige. The public image of the merchant that Molière exploited rather brutally in *Le bourgeois gentil-homme* was profoundly ignoble, and it afflicted the merchants themselves with feelings of inferiority that probably troubled them more than the contempt they actually encountered. To some extent their unhappiness was self-induced. . . . The merchants felt that the intense practical training of business, the constant supervision and attention it required, and its remoteness from the leisure and finesse of the proprietary round of life kept them from cultivating the social and intellectual qualities that brought respect. . . . Because these attitudes existed, anyone who remained in business, no matter how creditably he lived, suffered some discount in prestige. Even in the values of the Third Estate, diverse as they may have been, esteem was associated with proprietary wealth. Capitalism, which offered neither the assurance nor the standing that went with land and office, was simply a way, direct and dangerous, of getting rich.

The merchants, although they complained of the prejudices against trade, had to accept them as part of the status system and ground rules in the competition for standing. That is why they so often diverted profits into the purchase of country properties and offices, and why so many of them, once enriched, converted their commercial fortunes entirely into proprietary possessions. At an appropriate stage, the richest and most ambitious bought offices that conferred nobility. The members of the Danse family, linen merchants of Beauvais, constantly put business profits into country properties, acquired nobility, and, in 1757, liquidated their last partnership. During the Revolution, like other nobles and wealthy commoners, they lost their seigneurial dues, but purchased *biens nationaux* and remained until the Second Empire a family of provincial gentlemen. But this is only a sample of what was going on. The conversion of commercial capital into proprietary wealth was a regular feature of French history, from the sixteenth century to the eighteenth and even beyond. Apparently, the purpose of succeeding in business was to get the means of becoming a proprietor and a gentleman, and both Colbert and Necker, a century apart from one another, complained that this tendency drained off commerical and industrial capital and undermined economic growth. In order to counteract this, the government frequently authorized nobles to enter maritime and wholesale commerce and banking, thereby permitting ennobled merchants to continue in trade without losing status. This remedy, however, was only partly effective. It protected the juridical status of an ennobled merchant, but, since it had little impact on social values and attitudes, his sons were likely to drift into the administration, the armed forces, the judiciary, or country life, where sooner or later their ignoble origins would be forgotten.

There is no conclusive way of comparing the mass value of proprietary and business wealth in prerevolutionary France. Beginning with what passed in those days for statistics, supplementing them with estimates made by well-informed men who say little about their derivation, making inferences on assumptions which, though reasonable, can be endlessly debated, one concludes that the traditional modes of property—land, buildings, office, and *rentes*—accounted for more than 80 percent of French private wealth. This indicates a substantial preponderance for the proprietary sector. It is in no way aston-ishing. The day of heavy fixed industrial investment in factories and railroads, which would have altered the balance, lay far ahead. Meanwhile, most Frenchmen lived on the land, which yielded most of the taxable income and the gross national product. That is why the *économistes* not unreasonably attacked agricultural problems first, often to the neglect of the others.

For our purposes it is desirable to know the relative weight of the two kinds of capital not only for the society as a whole but in the upper Third Estate. Unfortunately, studies of the notarial records are not sufficiently advanced to show this. For the moment, all one can do is count persons, and from this it appears that even in the most heavily commercialized cities the proprietors and professional men in the Third Estate outnumbered the merchants. At Bor-deaux, the second most active port, there were 1,100 officials, professionals, *rentiers,* and property owners against only 700 merchants, brokers, and sugar refiners. At Rouen, a prime center of industry, banking, and maritime and wholesale trade, the administrative and judicial officers, professionals, and proprietors-*rentiers* outnumbered the merchants and brokers by more than three to one. At Toulouse, an agri-cultural, legal, and ecclesiastical capital, the ratio was about eleven to four, but the four included merchants who for the most part traded on small capital and in little volume and did much retail busi-ness, so that one hesitates to call them capitalists. There is, however, a further consideration. Because the merchants and industrialists owned, along with their commercial capital, considerable proprietary wealth, we could, with better data, divide them fractionally be-tween the two sectors, and, by such a pro-cedure, the share of commercial and industrial capital in the upper Third Estate would seem much lower than the impression we get by counting heads.

Soundings like these are merely straws in the wind, but they drift always in one direction. They confirm what seems to have been implicit in the con-sciousness of eighteenth-century France —that even in the well-to-do Third Estate proprietary wealth substantially outweighed commercial and industrial capital. This would not have surprised a Frenchman of the old regime and should not surprise us. The reason for stressing it here is to lay the ground for an assertion that is fundamental in analyzing the causes of the Revolution: there was, between most of the nobility and the proprietary sector of the middle classes, a continuity of investment forms and socioeconomic values that made them, economically, a single group. In the relations of production they played a common role. The differentiation be-tween them was not in any sense eco-nomic; it was juridical. . . . To sum up, there were nobles who were capitalists. There were merchants who were nobles. As the proprietary wealth traditionally identified with aristocracy extended far down into the Third Estate, so the capital-ism traditionally identified with the wealthy Third Estate penetrated into the second, and into its highest ranks.

This means that the old diagram by which we envision prerevolutionary society must be changed. There was a clear juridical boundary that separated nobles from commoners, and a commoner crossed it by registering a legal docu-ment, his letters of nobility. On the other hand, the frontier between capitalist and proprietary wealth ran vertically through both orders. The horizontal line marked a legal dichotomy, the vertical line, an economic one. To think of them as coinciding, even roughly, is to misunderstand the situation completely. The concept of two classes, at once economically and juridically disjunct, can be sustained only by ignoring the weight of proprietary wealth in the Third Estate and that of capitalism in the second, or, in other words, by continuing to ostracize them as unfacts.

From this follow two important conclusions. The first is that when the word bourgeois is used to indicate a nonnoble group playing a capitalist role in the relations of production it includes less than half the well-to-do Third Estate and excludes the proprietary groups that furnished 87 percent of the Third Estate deputation to the Estates-General. In other words, it embraces only a minority of the upper middle classes and explains almost nothing about the origins of the revolutionary leadership. In this sense it should be discarded as inadequate and misleading. But there are other senses, loaded with eighteenth-century implications, in which the word will continue to be employed because it alone translates what the documents have to say. One may, for example, speak of bourgeois who lived nobly on their revenues and comprised a fiscal category; these constituted a small portion of the Third Estate and counted entirely in the proprietary group. One may also speak of bourgeois as persons who, being inscribed in the registers of the bourgeoisie of a town, enjoyed what Anglo-Saxons call "the rights of the city," including political advantages and fiscal exemptions worth having, but in this sense the bourgeoisie included nobles and noncapitalist commoners and was not entirely of the Third Estate. Finally, one may adopt a peasant usage, applying the word bourgeois to townsmen who collected rents in and near the village and were felt to be an alien and adverse interest. All three meanings convey realities of the old regime and are useful on condition that one makes clear which of them he has in mind.

The second conclusion is that we have no economic explanation for the so-called "bourgeois revolution," the assault of the upper Third Estate on absolutism and aristocracy. No one denies that such an assault took place or that it left a powerful imprint upon French society. . . . By one of the unexamined postulates of current historiography we expect them to be explained by a conflict of social classes and the contradictions between a "rising" economic order and the order that it challenges. The position taken here is that we have now learned enough to see that this cannot be done, that to divide the wealthy elements of prerevolutionary society into a feudal aristocracy and a capitalist bourgeoisie forces the concealment of too much evidence, and that the whole classic concept of a bourgeois revolution has become impossible to sustain.

This leaves in our interpretation of the Revolution a somewhat painful void. Our instinct is to fill it with a new class struggle interpretation. . . . There may, however, be more plausibility in a political approach than in a reorganization of social categories. The gist of such an approach can be set down in two propositions. . . . First, the struggle against absolutism and aristocracy was the product of a financial and political crisis that it did not create. Second, it was essentially a political revolution with social consequences and not a social revolution with political consequences. . . .

The Revolution resulted from a bankruptcy that left the monarchy discredited and helpless. The disclosures of the first Assembly of Notables shocked everyone capable of reacting to public affairs, set off an expanding discussion of reforms, and raised hopes for a national regeneration. The government's reform program, which threatened privileges and seemed tainted with the supposed negligence and dishonesty of the Controller General Calonne, was rejected by the Notables. For more than a year the parlements and other constituted bodies opposed it. This resistance, the so-called *révolte nobiliaire*, taught the upper Third Estate the language, tactics, and gallantry of opposition. It made the convocation of the Estates-General inevitable. When in August 1788 this convocation was announced (along with a partial suspension of payments), there was thrust upon the nation a new political issue: whether royal power would pass to the privileged orders or would be shared with those who, until then, had been disfranchised. By inviting his subjects to advise him on how to organize the Estates-General, the King precipitated a landslide of publications that touched off a growing outcry for the doubling of the Third and the vote by head. This generated a political struggle between democracy . . . and aristocracy. . . . The stakes were very high. They included the question of at whose expense the financial problem would be solved, and whether careers in the military, the clergy, and the judiciary, and, above all, in politics would be opened to commoners, rich and poor, whose main resources were talents, education, and ambition. In explaining the democratic assault on despotism and aristocracy it is unnecessary to conjure up a social struggle rooted in economic change. The paralysis of the monarchy, the apprehensions of the taxable groups and creditors of the state, and the hopes and ambitions of the professional classes, combined with the slogans, myths, and images generated by the struggle, seem quite enough. . . .

ALFRED COBBAN (b. 1901), a distinguished English scholar, has raised some basic questions concerning the nature and impact of the Revolution. In this selection he deals with the fundamental problem of the scope and depth of the upheaval.*

Alfred Cobban

How Revolutionary Was the Revolution?

History, said Napoleon, is a myth that men agree to believe. I would rather say that it is this so long as it is something which it is important to them to believe or not. While the past lives it remains a myth, and naturally like all things living, it changes. The history of the French Revolution, whether garbed in the apocalyptic vision of a Carlyle or the profound scholarship of a Lefebvre, has continued to live and to change because it has continued to be bound up with the beliefs and aspirations of mankind.

I am tempted to suggest that in another sense also the French Revolution might be called a myth. At first, I must confess, I thought of entitling this lecture, "Was there a French Revolution?" However,

it seemed that to inaugurate this chair by eliminating the Revolution would be rather awkward; and it would certainly have been tactless to invite our French friends here and begin by abolishing their Revolution for them. I am therefore asking a safer question: "What was the French Revolution?" We used to think that it began in 1789. Now we know it began at least in 1787. It ended when? In 1815? Thiers and Aulard conclude their histories of the Revolution in 1799, Mathiez and Thompson in 1794, Guérin begins the reaction in 1793, Salvemini ends his history in 1792, and for some it has never ended. To each terminal date corresponds a different interpretation. Worse still follows. The Revolution has ceased to be a revolution and become a series of revolutions—the last Fronde of the nobles and the *parlements:* the revolution of the *tiers état,* the peasant rising, the republican insurrection, the revolt of the *sans-culottes,* the *neuf thermidor* and the various coups d'état under the Directory ending in that of 18 brumaire. The French Revolution is in fact a name we give to a long series of events. What it means depends on the light in which we see the connection between these events. In this sense the French Revolution, if not a myth, is a theory, or rather a number of rival theories.

Does this mean that before we can write it we need a philosophy of history? Certainly that would be one way out of the difficulty. A philosophy of history, like the beam of a searchlight, penetrates the obscurity of the recorded, and even better the unrecorded, past. It gives us the illusion that we are looking back along the path that humanity has followed to arrive at its present uneasy station and that unconscious forces or conscious will have determined that it should tread. But in truth the determination comes from us and is itself determined by the incidence of the light we are directing on the past. Change the angle only slightly and the beam may be lost in fog and mist, or a new set of facts swirl into clear light and an accepted theory die.

On the problem of historical causation de Tocqueville, as might be expected, makes one of the wisest observations:

I have lived with men of letters, who write history without ever being mixed up with practical affairs, and with politicians, who are only concerned with actual happenings, without ever thinking of describing them. I have always noticed that the former see only general causes, while the latter, living in the midst of the confusion of daily circumstances,

willingly imagine that everything can be reduced to a series of separate events, and that the petty strings which they are all the time pulling are those which move the world. It is to be believed that both the former and the latter are mistaken. For my part I hate those absolute systems which derive all the events in history from great first causes, link one to another in a chain of destiny, and, so to speak, eliminate men from history. I find them narrow in their pretended greatness, and false under their air of mathematical truth.

Yet the rule of chance in the great crises of history is one of the most difficult ideas for the human mind to tolerate. In a single separate event what we call chance or accident may be admitted; a universal, world-shaking movement such as the French Revolution seems to force determinism upon us. Historians of the Revolution, particularly of recent times, have increasingly tended to show why all that happened *had* to happen. The historian may not be able to see the strings which move his figures. It may be more interesting for him to pretend to forget them and describe his puppet play as though the actors moved of their own volition. But the really serious historian likes to think that this is make-believe, and prefers to concentrate on the mechanics of the process rather than on the mere twitches of arms and legs which simulate free action. But why should he stop at this? If there is one level of truth in the description of the movements of the puppets, and another in tracing the strings, the real historical causation, it is sometimes held, is to be found in the hidden forces that control them both. These are not to be seen but they may be deduced, as the Greeks detected the vagaries of the inhabitants of Olympus behind the changing destinies of their clients and victims here below. Of course, the new Olympus is infinitely more respectable. The wanton favours and enmities of a pack of uninhibited gods and goddesses no longer bring superhuman success or inhuman punishment. Great impersonal forces have taken their place, or rather a single great impersonal force, which is there operating unseen all the time, though only when there is a great revolution in human destinies, we are told, do we become fully aware of its ceaseless inexorable working, before which one social order passes away and in the predetermined pattern of history, another emerges.

To pass from the general to the particular, in the French Revolution, it is commonly said, the feudal order passed away and the rule of the bourgeoisie took its place. This is, put simply, the myth which has dominated serious research on the history of the French Revolution during the present century. It is often treated as an exemplification of a scientific law derived from the facts of history. If I am calling it a myth, this is in no derogatory sense but in a Platonic way of speaking, which may, of course, be worse. The fact that it has come to be taken for granted is my reason for re-examining it. Simplifying, but then this is essentially a *conte de fées,* the outline of the story is that there was once a social order called feudalism. This was a terrible ogre and lived in a castle; but for centuries a bourgeois Jack the Giant-killer climbed the beanstalk of economic progress, until finally in the French Revolution he liquidated the old order and put in its place something called alternatively bourgeois society or capitalism. The only divergence from the traditional story is that he did not live happily ever after. I think it would be fair to say that this is the generally ac-

cepted myth or theory of the French Revolution, and of course both the factors in it are themselves theories. I propose to discuss them in turn.

The first is feudalism. This is a term that was invented to describe the social organization that prevailed in the Middle Ages. By the time of the French Revolution, as a system of government based on the ownership of land it had long come to an end in France. Not only had the feudal aristocracy ceased to govern the country, it had even ceased to own a large part of the land. A rough estimate is that one-third of the land had passed into the possession of the peasantry, and a fair proportion of the remainder was forest or waste. The so-called feudalism of the eighteenth century consisted in the survival of antiquated dues and services owed to the descendants of the former feudal seigneurs, or to those who had purchased their *seigneuries*. A considerable body of *feudistes* lived out of the continual law-suits that these claims, registered in *terriers,* involved. In the years before 1789 an attempt was made by the possessors of feudal rights—and possibly in particular by their new possessors, though this is a matter that requires investigation—to revive old ones that had long fallen into disuse and to enforce surviving ones more rigorously. In spite of this, they remained a peculiarly functionless survival, the relics of an atrophied organ, which only a very adventurous social biologist could use to justify a classification with some fossil feudal order of the past. In the words of a legal historian, the fief, in the eighteenth century, was "une forme bizarre de propriété foncière". The jurists of the time admitted that the "seigneur utile," that is to say the *tenancier,* was the real proprietor, though his property involved certain obligations, which they described in legal terminology as a "servitude au profit du seigneur foncier."

How little the so-called feudal dues deserved their title was to be proved in the course of the attempt to apply the decrees of August 4th–11th, 1789, by which the Constituent Assembly proposed to abolish those dues that were feudal in origin, while at the same time maintaining those payments or services which were of the nature of economic rent. It proved impossible to make the distinction in practice, and after years of legal struggle the attempt was abandoned and all dues which qualified ownership disappeared. This was just what the Constituent Assembly had feared and tried to avoid, for to suggest that the members of the Assembly wanted to abolish dues which many of them had acquired themselves would be a mistake. On the contrary, their disappearance was an unlooked-for and unwanted by-product of the Revolution. The night of the Fourth of August was not quite the spontaneous and generous gesture it has been made to seem. The men of property who sat in the Constituent Assembly, as Professor Lefebvre has pointed out, could not approve of confiscatory methods of dealing with property, especially when some of it was their own. The countryside took matters into its own hands when it broke out in the last jacquerie, under the stimulus of economic distress, the excitement of the drawing up of the *cahiers* and the election of the *tiers état,* and the general breakdown of authority resulting from the *révolte nobiliaire.* The unrest in the spring and summer of 1789 was so widespread that a major military operation would have been necessary to suppress it. The night of the Fourth of August was an attempt by throwing overboard

some of the dues to salvage the rest. In the age of Reason, feudal went with such terms of abuse as Gothic and medieval. If the property rights that were sacrificed were called feudal, this was at least in part to prevent the episode from becoming a precedent in respect of other property rights. It was necessary to give the dog a bad name in order to justify his having been hanged. But the peasantry did not draw such subtle legal distinctions. They simply ceased to pay their dues, whatever their nature, and no subsequent government had the strength to make them resume payment. In the words of Lefebvre, "they liberated themselves, and the successive Assemblies only sanctioned what they had accomplished." If the system of seigneurial rights can be identified with the medieval social order called feudal; and if the reluctant acceptance of a *fait accompli* by the Constituent Assembly can be called abolishing feudalism, then, I suppose, the first part of the prevailing myth of the Revolution can hold good. The qualifications seem to be so extensive as to make the statement practically meaningless.

What of the other factor in the theory, the revolt of the bourgeoisie? It is unnecessary nowadays to labour the point that the Revolution began as an aristocratic rising; the Counter-revolution, as it subsequently became, in fact preceded the Revolution by at least two years. It has been described as the last Fronde and it marked the ultimate failure of Louis XIV's effort to place the monarchy so far above the privileged classes that they could never again challenge its authority as they had done during his minority. Of set purpose he had excluded the old *noblesse* from positions of authority in the state. Under the *grand monarque* the son of an official of Rouen, Colbert, could become the greatest man in the realm after the king, while only one of the highest nobles was allowed in a ministerial office. Under his weaker successors the Court took its revenge and nobles infiltrated into the government of the state. They monopolized the higher ranks of the Church and the Army, filled the *Conseil d'en haut* and supplied occupants for nearly all the ministries except that of the Controller General. The calling of the Assembly of Notables was a tacit recognition that the king could not govern against the will of the privileged orders, but instead of gaining their support he found that by giving them an organ of self-expression he had merely opened the flood-gates of aristocratic revolt.

The last of the Frondes was in appearance a formidable movement. In reality it was an attempt by a class of parasites to take over the body politic, which they possessed the power to destroy but not to recreate. It was a revolt of the drones, for though nobles might occupy places of influence and power, the one thing the *noblesse* as a class did not do was work. There were, of course, exceptions, but, by and large, the *noblesse de race* had no field of active service to the state except the Army, in which its numbers and courage did not make up for its indiscipline and inefficiency. French society had become etiolated, and if it could still produce fine flowers at the top, it was at the expense of the health of the whole plant. Nobles occupied positions of dignity and remuneration, the Court *noblesse* relied for its finances increasingly on the profits of places and pensions, but nearly all the effective business of the state was done by men a grade lower down. In the embassies one finds that *chargés* or secretaries, emerging from lower social strata, often performed most of the real work of diplomacy. In the

généralités the duties of the *intendants* —now almost invariably noble even if their nobility was sometimes of rather recent vintage—were increasingly falling into the hands of the *secrétaire de l'intendance* and the *subdélégués,* as was shown by the fact that *intendants* themselves sometimes stayed away from their *généralités* for long periods. The ministries in Paris were dependent on the work of their permanent officials. The efficient officers in the Army were largely those whose social origins prevented them from rising to the higher ranks. The legal work of France was carried out not by some thousand proud *parlementaires* but by a host of minor judicial officers. From commerce the *noblesse* was generally excluded under penalty of *dérogeance;* and though it was easy for wealthy *roturiers* to pass into the ranks of the *noblesse,* they could only do so by abandoning their effective functions and *vivant noblement.* Some nobles, or at least *ennoblis,* might be found as exceptions to these statements, but as a broad generalization it may be said that it was all those who did the real work of administering France who formed the *tiers état.* These men were drawn from and constituted an important, perhaps even the greatest, element in the bourgeoisie: and this brings me to the second of my problems, for bourgeois is a term used almost as loosely as feudalism.

In Great Britain we commonly think of the rise of the bourgeoisie as the rise of that class which was primarily concerned with the control of trade, industry and finance, as composed therefore of merchants, bankers, industrialists and capitalists, great and small. The accepted theory of the French Revolution is that it came when the new form of property which such men represented replaced the older form represented by the feudal landowners. Is this a correct analysis? I must begin by premising that if it was a revolt of the "monied men," to use Burke's term, it was certainly not provoked by economic grievances. The fine eighteenth-century quarters of French provincial towns are standing evidence of the wealth of the men who built them, as well as of the standards of taste that dictated their elegance. However, it is hardly necessary to discuss the reasons they might, or might not, have had for making a revolution until we are quite sure that they made it. Now, in fact, the men who made the Revolution of 1789 were the members of the Constituent Assembly; little of what had been achieved by 1791 was to be lost, and most of what was done subsequently was to be undone. The essential first question to ask, then, is who formed the *tiers état* of 1789?

Were they the representatives of a rising industrial capitalist class? To imagine that this was even possible would be to antedate such industrial revolution as France was to experience by more than half a century. Some kind of clue to their importance in society will be provided if we ask how many manufacturers there were among those elected in 1789. Those who actually sat in the Assembly, either as deputies or *suppléants,* in the *tiers état,* numbered 648. Among these there were just eight who are described as manufacturers or *maîtres de forges.* Perhaps, however, the bourgeois were the merchants? Some 76 of the *tiers* are described as *marchands* or *négociants.* Only about 20 of these came from places of any commerical importance; the remainder should perhaps be regarded primarily as local notables. Very few of them seem to have played any prominent part in the Revolution. The world of finance produced one solitary banker,

though one merchant also described himself as a banker. Together, merchants, manufacturers and financiers amount to 85, or 13 per cent of the whole number.

If they were not merchants or manufacturers, then, what were the *tiers état* of 1789? The category of those concerned with trade and industry is easy to identify. The social status or function of the others is apt to be more difficult to distinguish, sometimes for lack of sufficient indication—"bourgeois vivant noblement" is fairly easy to place, as is even "citoyen"; but what is the significance of "bourgeois fils aîné"? Sometimes there appears also that great handicap which the modern historian suffers from as compared with the historian of medieval or ancient times, too much information. How is one to classify a member (of the Convention) described as "landowner, leather manufacturer, lawyer and professor of mathematics and physics"? My figures are, therefore, all approximate, but I do not think that a variation of a few either way would do much to alter the general picture that emerges of the kind of men who composed the *tiers état* of 1789.

It is usually said that the majority were lawyers. This is undoubtedly true, but it is not as illuminating a statement as might be supposed. True, we can make out an impressive list of well over 400 lawyers in the Constituent Assembly, but this description tells us little about their actual social status or functions. It is as useful as would be a contemporary social classification based on the possession of a university degree.

Fortunately we know something more about most of the members. Those who are described as lawyers *(avocats* or *notaires)* without any further qualification number 166, just about a quarter and it might be held that this was quite enough for the health of the Assembly. The remainder of the huge legal contingent falls into a different category. It includes members of the *ministère public,* notaries royal, local judges, municipal officers, and above all *lieutenants généraux* of *bailliages* and *sénéchaussées.* It may be observed in passing that there was an extraordinary number of officers of *bailliage* and *sénéchaussée* among those elected, which is perhaps not unconnected with the fact that these areas formed the constituencies. Add to these the various officials of the state services—25—and the total of 278 is reached, that is some 43 per cent of the whole membership.

To describe these men simply as lawyers is to ignore one of the essential features of the *ancien régime.* It would be almost as justifiable as a social analysis which classified the Justices of the Peace in England primarily as lawyers, for as late as the eighteenth century administration and justice were inextricably mixed up in most countries. The great majority of the so-called lawyers were in fact juridico-administrative officers, holding *charges* in municipality or *bailliage* or one of the state services. These were nearly always venal posts, which went therefore to those with a sufficient competence to pay the purchase price, unless they were lucky enough to inherit them from a relation. Thus in 1789 the office of notary could cost as much as three or four hundred thousand *livres* in Paris; in the provinces it might be worth much less.

An office or *charge* was an investment, a status and a job. Those who bought them were not spending their money for nothing; they drew in return a commensurate income from fees. How much work they had to do for it must remain a matter of doubt: the number of office-holders is evidence of the financial needs of the Crown, rather than of the administrative needs of the country. One little *bourg* of 3,000 inhabitants in the seventeenth century rejoiced in a *bailli,* a *prévot,* a *lieutenant,* a *procureur fiscal,* six notaries, four *sergents,* twelve *procureurs,* and four *greffiers.* Doubtless they also served the surrounding countryside, but it seems a lot. It is difficult not to suspect that, whatever their fees, they were overpaid for their services. They could reply, of course, that having bought their jobs they were entitled to a return on their investment.

The presence of such a large proportion of venal officers in the Constituent Assembly is at first sight difficult to reconcile with the holocaust of their offices effected by the Assembly itself, apparently with little protest. One can understand that they were ready to sacrifice the privileges of the *noblesse* and the clergy, but that an important part of their own income should have gone the same way appears at first sight to indicate a spirit of self-sacrifice and idealism rarely to be predicated of the average political man. We need not, however, in this case hypothesize any superhuman virtue. The venal offices were abolished, it is true, but not without compensation. Admittedly, the compensation was in *assignats:* but no one as yet knew, or dreamed of, the depths to which the *assignat* was to fall. Those who clung to their paper money long enough doubtless lost it all; but it is permissible to suppose that many rapidly reinvested their compensation. It would be interesting to know to what extent the payment for the venal offices was used for the purchase of the nationalized lands of the Church. Certainly the coincidence by which the venal officers, who formed such an important element in the Constituent Assembly, obtained a large supply of free capital, just at the time when an unprecedented opportunity for its investment in land was opened to them, was a very happy one.

It need not be assumed that there were no other motives, of a more disinterested nature, involved in the treatment of the venal offices. But though the demands of a more efficient administration called for their abolition, the venal officers had no occasion to feel that their posts were contrary to social morality. They were all, in a sense, living on the state; but if they looked higher up the social scale they could see plenty who held places and pensions by favour of the Court, without having had to pay for them, or having to do any work in them at all. In their monopoly of the positions combining the maximum of remuneration with the minimum of duties, the privileged orders had something more valuable than a mere decorative social superiority, and the bourgeois a substantial grievance.

Thiers, who was close to the Revolution and knew many of its participants, held that if the Crown had established some equality in official appointments and given some guarantees, the major source of discontent would have been eliminated. De Tocqueville, a little later, put forward a similar view of the revolution of 1848. "If many of the conservatives," he wrote, "only defended the Ministry with the aim of keeping their salaries and jobs, I must say that many of the opposition only appeared to me to be attacking it in order to get jobs for themselves. The truth, a deplorable truth, is that the taste for official jobs and the desire to live on the taxes is not with us the peculiar malady of a particular party, it is the great and permanent infirmity of the nation itself" — "C'est le mal secret, qui a rongé tous

les anciens pouvoirs et qui rongera de même tous les nouveaux."

De Tocqueville, I think, was mistaken only in supposing that this was peculiarly a cause of revolution in France. I suspect that it has a broader application to other revolutions.

A comparison with England in the eighteenth century is not unilluminating here, if one considers the differing prospects that offered themselves to men of ability, lacking what is in all societies so much more valuable than mere ability—money and family influence—in the England and in the France of the eighteenth century. A Robespierre, a Danton, a Vergniaud, in France before 1789 could not hope to be anything but the kind of petty attorney on whom Burke poured scorn. In England at the same time, Vergniaud would have shone as an orator in the House of Commons, to which his talents would undoubtedly have carried him, even in the company of Fox and Sheridan. It is not difficult to envisage Danton as a future Lord Chancellor. The more modest talents of Robespierre would doubtless have been satisfied with the post of Lord Chief Justice, if he could have reconciled holding such a post with his objections to capital punishment. Fouché might have become Archbishop of Canterbury, Roland would have been a simple under-secretary of state and member of parliament, but the opportunities that such a post provided for mixing in high society and being received at Court would probably have contented that sentimental little salon politician, Madame Roland. Lord Chancellor Eldon and the great international lawyer, Lord Stowell, sons of a Tyneside keelman and an innkeeper, had no better start than any of these; nor did Thurlow, son of a country vicar. A measure of unscrupulousness, combined with eloquence and political ability, brought him to the Woolsack. Similar qualities only brought Danton to the guillotine. In France, if he had ever had sufficient assiduity to accumulate the necessary money, Thurlow might have become president of a *grenier à sel*, perhaps even *avocat au parlement*, hardly more.

The Church under Louis XVI had not a single bishop who was not noble by birth. In England, John Potter, son of a draper, and obtaining his education as servitor at Oxford, could become Archbishop of Canterbury. Isaac Maddox, orphan and apprenticed to a pastrycook, ended up as a bishop, as did Richard Watson, son of a country schoolteacher. The Navy—though not the Army—offered another opening for men of talent to rise to the top. One cannot but ask oneself what would have happened to the Revolution in France if in a similar way so many of those who were to be its leaders had in advance been absorbed into the ranks of power and prestige. Whatever else the *tiers état* of 1789 wanted, they certainly wanted "la carrière ouverte aux talents."

Returning to the analysis of the revolutionary bourgeoisie, it may be said that the Revolution did not end with the Constituent Assembly, and that its subsequent developments brought, in the Convention, another set of men into power. An analysis of the membership of the Convention gives results which naturally vary from those for the Constituent Assembly. The financial, mercantile and manufacturing section is even smaller—83 out of 891, some 9 per cent. Lawyers are present in about the same proportion of one-fourth. Office holders are down from 43 to 25 percent, though as the venal offices were now a thing of the past, it is unlikely that this figure represents all those who had held such positions under the *ancien régime*. A tiny group of *petits bourgeois* and ordinary soldiers appears, to offset which we have rather more nobles and colonial proprietors. There are more clergy, of course, now that they have no Order of their own. The most notable development is the appearance of a substantial group of what one might call professional men in addition to the lawyers: 32 professors or teachers, some of them also clerics; 58 doctors, surgeons or pharmacists; some lower officers of the Army, the Navy and merchant marine; a few writers and actors. Altogether this category has risen from about 5 percent to 17 percent.

Like the *Constituante*, the Convention is still almost exclusively a bourgeois assembly, and in 1792, as in 1789, bourgeois has to be interpreted in the sense of a class of *fonctionnaires* and professional men. Admittedly, its actions were not the same as those of the *Constituante*. Under pressure from the popular movement in Paris, and amid the storm and stress of counter-revolution and war, policies were accepted by a purged Convention which, as is the way of revolutions, after the purgers had themselves been purged, it was to repudiate. These surface storms of the Revolution are not my subject. When they had died down, and under Napoleon it was possible to make some calculation as to who had emerged in triumph, it could be seen that the smaller fry had mostly continued to inhabit the shallows, while the officials and the professional men of the *ancien régime*, mixed with a fair number of former nobles and a few able men from the ranks, had emerged as the governing class of the new regime.

Once again figures tell the story better than words. Of the members of the Constituent Assembly and the Convention, 111 held high office, and 518 lower offices, under Napoleon, and of these over one-third had held office before 1789. Both Assemblies contained many obscure men who subsequently sank back into the obscurity from which they had emerged. They contained more than a few who, republican by principle, refused to accept the Empire and the share in the fruits of office which they might otherwise have had. There were also the liquidations, the method by which revolutions solve the problem of too many people pursuing too few jobs. But in the end it may have been that a fair proportion of those who had given up their venal offices for compensation at the beginning of the Revolution obtained new ones that were free from the stigma of venality at the end. It may at least be suggested as an hypothesis worthy of investigation that the essence of government in France after the Revolution remained where it had been before, in the great and now renewed bureaucratic *cadres*. With Napoleon returned the *Conseil d'État,* to resume the functions of the councils that had formerly surrounded the throne. Since then, assemblies and emperors and kings have come and gone, but the *Conseil d'État* and the *maîtres des requêtes* have remained at the apex of the administrative pyramid and provided the lasting structure of government behind a series of changing regimes.

It may seem that as a result of this interpretation the Revolution is reduced considerably in scope, that everything that survived after 1799 had already been gained by 1791. Essentially this is, I think, true, but how, then, account for eight years of disorder and continuing revolution? One answer that is often given is

to attribute it to the struggle against the counter-revolution. I suspect that this is to give too much weight to a movement that was moribund from birth; but the myth of the counter-revolution is not my subject here. The war was, I believe, a more important factor, but that also is another subject.

The Revolution began from above, but it was continued by pressure from below. This did not come from the peasantry, who achieved their objective at an early stage and after that ceased to have any active interest in the Revolution beyond safeguarding their gains. But in the towns the poorer population suffered increasingly from inflation and the shortage of supplies, and constituted, therefore, a source of potential unrest which could be exploited by the political factions. If it had been calculated—which of course it was not—for the perpetuation of a revolutionary situation, the system of inflation could not have been better chosen. But when it came to an end the difference between 1799 and 1791 was far less than that between 1791 and 1789.

If I have put forward the view that the interpretation of the Revolution as the substitution of a capitalist bourgeois order for feudalism is a myth, this is not to suggest that the Revolution itself is mythical and that nothing of significance happened in France at this time. The revolutionaries drew a line at the end of the *ancien régime,* subtracted the negative factors from the past, and added up the sum of what was positive, to be carried forward on the next page. A class of officials and professional men moved up from the minor to the major posts in government and dispossessed the minions of an effete Court: this was what the bourgeois revolution meant. The peasants relieved themselves of their seigneurial dues: this was the meaning of the abolition of feudalism. But even taken together these two developments hardly constitute the abolition of one social order and the substitution of another for it, and if the accepted theory is not quite a myth, it seems singularly like one.

Did the Revolution effect no more fundamental change than this? In French economy it might be considered that it held back rather than encouraged changes which were to come much later and are still very incomplete. Politically it replaced the divine right of the king by the divine right of the people. In theory this was to substitute an absolute power for one limited by its nature, and to eliminate the rights of the people as against a government which was henceforth theoretically themselves. The war dictatorship of the Committee of Public Safety, and the Napoleonic Empire, were the historical if not the logical sequel to the assertion of the sovereignty of the people. But this aspect of the Revolution has perhaps been unduly emphasized of late. Sovereignty remained sovereignty, whether exercised in the name of God or the people, even though the Revolution changed both the possessors and the nature of power in the state.

I implied, earlier in this lecture, that the Revolution was not one but many. One of the greatest of its aspects I have so far neglected. Men have ideas, whatever those historians who have tried to decerebrate history may say, and these ideas are not to be treated merely as the expression of material interests. The explanation of the causation of the Revolution simply in terms of the ideas of the eighteenth century has long been discarded from serious history, but this not to say that the revolutionaries were mere economic animals to be summed up in terms of the stud book and the bank balance, or reduced to a number of holes punched in an index card. The members of the French revolutionary assemblies had been bred on the ideas of the Enlightenment. Reforms such as the abolition of torture in legal proceedings and many other legal changes, or the removal of the disabilities of Protestants and Jews, are not to be explained in terms of material interests. But here again, though the Revolution may have accelerated some of these reforms, it perhaps put back others. Here also the historian has to admit not only that these reforms were the children of the ideas of the eighteenth century, but that their implementation had already begun before 1789. The reign of Louis XVI was an age of reform, which the Revolution continued. The armies of the Revolution and Napoleon, it has been said, spread the humanitarian ideal of the eighteenth century to the rest of Europe, strange missionaries though they were. There is some truth in this, though if we consider the development of subsequent history we may be tempted to think that the seeds of the Enlightenment, east of the Rhine and south of the Alps and the Pyrenees, fell on very stony ground. The main point I want to make, however, is that whether we analyse the revolutionary age in terms of social forces or of ideas, it appears more and more clearly as the child of the eighteenth century and only to be understood in terms of the society out of which it emerged. To interpret the Revolution we must look back as well as forward, and forget if possible that 1789 has ever seemed a date from which to begin.

But here I am myself falling into the error of speaking as though there were a single French Revolution, to be summed up in a single formula. This conception, whatever theory it is enshrined in, is the real fallacy behind all the myths of the French Revolution—the idea that there was *a* French Revolution, which you can be for or against. If in some respects the revolutionaries gave expression to the ideas of the Enlightenment, in others they undermined their application; for they stood between the rational and the romantic ages, between the Enlightenment and the religious revival, between a great wave of humanitarian sentiment and the Terror, between the oecumenical ideal and the rise of nationalism, between the idealism of 1789 and the cynicism of the Directory, between the proclamation of universal brotherhood and the wars of Napoleon. They reached the heights of heroism and descended to the depths of civil strife. A whole generation packed with significance for good and evil is summed up in the phrase "the French Revolution." We may pick out what we admire or dislike in it and call that the Revolution, but either is a partial verdict. Its significance in the world today is such that we must take all its aspects, for good or for bad, into consideration in our contemporary world-picture. The great school of French historians which has enlarged our knowledge of the revolutionary age has driven farther away the boundaries at which ultimate disagreement begins; but no single historian, and neither contemporaries nor any succeeding generation, has ever grasped the whole of the revolutionary age in a single all-embracing view. Every interpretation of the Revolution must in the nature of things be partial, and every partial view is a myth.

Using the techniques of sociology, GEORGE RUDÉ (b. 1910), a British historian, has studied revolutionary crowds. He has sought to discover who joined the insurrectionary mobs and to clarify their motives.*

George Rudé

Who Joined a Revolutionary Mob?

For all their diversity of scope, organization, and design, does a common thread run through the various revolutionary commotions and *journées* described in the preceding pages? In the first place, it is evident that there is a certain uniformity of pattern in the social composition of the participants in these movements: with the single exception of the armed rebels of Vendémiaire, they were drawn in their overwhelming majority from the Parisian *sans-culottes*—from the workshop masters, craftsmen, wage-earners, shopkeepers, and petty traders of the capital. Thus, in respect of social origins, a sharp division is revealed between the mass of demonstrators and insurgents and the political leaders directing, or

making political capital out of, these operations—the Paris Electors of May–July 1789, the revolutionary journalists, the leaders of the Paris Commune, or the members of the National Assembly, of the Cordeliers and Jacobin Clubs. These, with remarkably few exceptions, were drawn from the commercial *bour-geoisie*, the professions, or the liberal aristocracy. . . .

Yet, though overwhelmingly composed of *sans-culottes*, the revolutionary crowds taking part in these events were by no means drawn from identical social groups. It would, in fact, be a gross over-simplification to present them as a sort of homogeneous, nameless "mob" of the lower orders of Parisian society ever ready to

---

*George Rudé, *The Crowd in the French Revolution* (Oxford: Clarendon Press, 1959), pp. 178–190. Footnotes omitted.

spring into action at the behest of political leaders or in spontaneous response to the promptings of hunger or of momentary grievance. Yet such has only too often been the picture of them that has emerged from the pen of the memorialist or historian.

To correct this picture we shall have to consider the motives underlying the revolutionary *journées;* but, before doing so, we must also look once more at the elements taking part in them. The riots of the autumn of 1787 and 1788 broke out, as we saw, in response to the agitation of the Paris *Parlement* in the course of its struggle with the king and his ministers in the period of the *révolte nobiliaire.* The original impulse to them was given by the lawyers' clerks and ushers of the Palais de Justice; yet, as the riots continued, the clerks were joined by the apprentices and journeymen of the Cité and, in 1788, by the *menu peuple* of the markets and the Faubourgs Saint-Marcel and Saint-Germain as well. In fact those arrested were composed, in the main, of small shopkeepers, craftsmen, and journeymen, of whom one-half were wage-earners in a variety of trades. Workshop journeymen and labourers played an even more conspicuous part in the Réveillon riots of April 1789, when the houses of two manufacturers were pulled down by angry crowds in the Faubourg Saint-Antoine. We saw that, on this occasion, special efforts were made by the itinerant bands, who formed the most active elements among the rioters, to enrol wage-earners both at their places of work—at docks, in workshops and manufactories—and in their lodgings; and wage-earners of every sort accounted for over fifty of some seventy persons killed, wounded, or arrested as a result of the disturbances. While this is an unusually high proportion, it is perhaps not surprising in view of the particular hostility aroused among the journeymen and labourers of the *faubourg* and its approaches by the threats that Réveillon had, either by implication or design, uttered against the workers' living standards at a time of acute shortage and high price of bread.

In a very real sense it may be claimed that the Paris revolution of July 1789 was the work of a great part of the population as a whole: those under arms, may, as we have seen, have numbered as many as a quarter of a million. Yet the most active elements in the main episodes of that great upsurge were far fewer and are reasonably well known to us. The immediate assailants of the Bastille, most of whom were members of the newly formed National Guard, were only a few hundred in number. While a handful of these were prosperous merchants or other *bourgeois,* the great majority were craftsmen, shopkeepers, and journeymen, drawn from a wide variety of trades and occupations, though predominantly from the building, furnishing, and luxury crafts of the Faubourg Saint-Antoine and its adjoining districts. At the Bastille, the unemployed country-workers, whose influx into the capital had been one of the more striking manifestations of the economic crisis which heralded the Revolution, played little or no part; and wage-earners in general, even workshop journeymen, appear to have been in a distinct minority. Quite different was the composition of the crowds that burned down the customs posts between 11 and 14 July and raided and sacked the monastery of the Saint-Lazare brotherhood on the 13th. At the *barrières,* as at the Bastille, there was a small number of *bourgeois*—even of nobles—among the most prominent of the insurgents. . . . Yet these were exceptional and the description most often given of the rioters by eyewitnesses was of roughly dressed men and women of the people—local trades-men, craftsmen and wage-earners, among whom wine-merchants and allegedly pro-fessional smugglers were much in evi-dence, but also working housewives, water-carriers, building and barrel workers, and unemployed.... At the Saint-Lazare monastery, too, the work of looting and destruction seems, in the main, to have been carried out by small tradesmen, employed and unemployed labourers, and local poor rather than by craftsmen and journeymen. This was, of course, unlike the two other episodes, a purely local affair and the persons taking part in it were almost all resident in an area adjoining the junction of the rue du Faubourg Saint-Denis and the rue du Faubourg Saint-Lazare on the northern outskirts of the city.

In the case of the march to Versailles on 5 October, which brought Louis XVI back to his capital, there are no lists of participants to enlighten us, and the po-lice reports on those arrested and killed are far too few in number to make it pos-sible to draw any general conclusions from them. Yet we know from Hardy's *Journal* and from the testimony of various other reporters and witnesses that the women of the markets both initiated the whole movement for bread in September and October and played the predominant part in the first great contingent that set out for Versailles; but we have also noted that the women marchers included, in addition to the petty, privileged stall-holders, fish-wives and working women of the markets, well-dressed *bourgeoises* ... and other women of various social classes.... We know a great deal less about the 20,000 *gardes nationaux* that paraded in the Place de Grève that morn-ing and compelled the apparently re-luctant Lafayette to lead them to Ver-sailles later in the evening in the wake of the marching women—but it appears from the evidence given by witnesses before the Paris Châtelet and from the handful of arrests made at Versailles that they were once more composed of the workshop masters, craftsmen, and jour-neymen of the Faubourg Saint-Antoine and its adjoining districts. Yet pride of place, on this occasion, undoubtedly goes to the stall-holders and fish-wives of the central markets. In this event, more than in any other similar event in the Revolu-tion, women played the leading part and held the centre of the stage throughout.

After the prolonged lull of 1790 . . . the popular movement, fed by the agitation of the democrats and the Cordeliers Club, started up again in the spring of 1791. This time it became more widespread, involving probably every one of the Paris Sections, and took on a distinctly political form. Its culmination was the meeting round the *autel de la patrie*[1] in the Champ de Mars on 17 July 1791, when 50,000 people gathered to sign a petition drawn up by the Cordeliers Club, calling for the abdication of Louis XVI. Of the 6,000 persons who had signed the petition be-fore martial law was declared and the Garde Nationale opened fire, a great number could neither read nor write and the petition sheets were studded with circled crosses in the place of sig-natures. From the indirect evidence of the police reports we learn that of some 250 persons arrested on political charges during the summer and autumn months, or wounded or killed in the demon-stration itself, a little over half were wage-earners, the rest being mainly self-employed craftsmen, shopkeepers, and petty traders, with a sprinkling of

---

[1] Altar of the nation.—Ed.

rentiers, bourgeois, professional men, and clerks; about one in twenty were women.

The assault on the Tuileries in August 1792 was, like that on the Bastille two years earlier, a largely military affair and was carried out by organized battalions of the Parisian National Guard, supported by visiting contingents from a number of provincial cities. As wage-earners had been virtually excluded from the Paris militia until a few days previously and as women would only in exceptional cases be enrolled, we should not expect the insurgents of 10 August to be as broadly representative of the Parisian *sans-culottes* as a whole as those involved in the political movement of 1791. Yet, from the lists of those applying for pensions for themselves or their dependents, we have seen that once more it was the *sans-culottes* of the *faubourgs* and markets that played the principal role: of 123 persons whose occupations appear on these lists, the great majority were craftsmen, shopkeepers, journeymen, and "general" workers, wage-earners accounting for about two-fifths of the total.

As far as we can tell from incomplete records, the crowds taking part in the food riots of the early months of 1792 and 1793 were of a somewhat different complexion. These were, it may be remembered, more or less spontaneous outbursts directed against provision merchants, particularly grocers, at times of steeply rising prices. Not surprisingly, women were much in evidence in these disturbances: grocers' depositions spoke of cohorts of women invading their shops, and laundresses and market-women of the Faubourg Saint-Marcel were picked out for special mention. One woman, Agnès Bernard by name, was sentenced to two years' prison for her part in the riots of 1793; yet the number of women actually arrested—about one in eight of the prisoners—does not fully reflect the part played by them in these episodes. Another feature was the comparatively large number of cooks and domestic servants that were involved; and of the wage-earners arrested (some three-fifths of those appearing in the records), the majority were, in fact, servants, porters, and other unskilled or general workers rather than journeymen of the traditional crafts.

Both women and craftsmen reappear in large numbers in the great popular revolt against Robespierre's Thermidorian successors in Prairial of the Year III (May 1795). In this respect there is a remarkable resemblance between this outbreak and that of October 1789, when Parisians marched to Versailles with the double object of protesting against the shortage of bread and of bringing the king back to the capital. In both cases the women of the markets and *faubourgs* played a significant part and an insurrection of tradesmen and craftsmen enrolled in battalions of the National Guard followed closely on the heels of a women's revolt for bread. In the case of Prairial this feature is reflected in the lists of civilians arrested for taking part in the disturbances: alongside a substantial minority of women we find a prevalence of workshop masters, independent craftsmen, and journeymen of a wide variety of trades.

From this brief review we may note both the common feature and certain significant differences in the composition of the rioters and insurgents of this period. The common feature is, of course, the predominance of *sans-culottes* in all but one of these *journées*. Yet other social elements played some part: overwhelmingly so in Vendémiaire of the Year IV;

but there were also small groups of *bourgeois, rentiers,* merchants, civil servants, and professional men engaged in the destruction of the *barrières* (possibly as direct agents of the Orleanist faction at the Palais Royal), in the capture of the Bastille, the Champ de Mars affair, the assault on the Tuileries, and in the outbreak of Prairial. Women, as we have seen, were particularly in evidence in the march to Versailles, the food riots of 1792–3, and in Prairial. This is, of course, not altogether surprising, as in these episodes food prices and other bread and butter questions were well to the fore; we find women playing a less conspicuous part in such an essentially political movement as that culminating in the "massacre" of the Champ de Mars—less still, of course, in largely military operations like the assaults on the Bastille and the Tuileries and in the expulsion of the Girondin deputies from the Convention. Again, while wage-earners played a substantial part on all these occasions, the only important outbreak in which they appear to have clearly predominated was the Réveillon riots in the Faubourg Saint-Antoine. The reason for this is not hard to find: though it cannot be termed a strike or a wages movement (Réveillon's own workers do not appear to have been engaged), it was the only one of these actions in which there is the slightest trace of a direct conflict between workers and employers. It is also no doubt significant that craftsmen—whether masters, independent craftsmen, or journeymen— were more conspicuously in evidence in some of the *journées* than in others. This seems particularly to have been the case when a district of small crafts became substantially involved—like the Cité in the riots of 1787 and 1788 or the Faubourg Saint-Antoine on various other occasions; but it also appears to have been

a feature of the more organized, political movements—such as the Champ de Mars affair and the armed attacks on the Bastille and the Tuileries—when the driving element was no doubt the small shopkeepers and workshop masters who, in many cases, brought their *garçons,* journeymen, and apprentices along with them. In this connexion it is perhaps of interest to note the sustained militancy of members of certain trades such as furnishing, building, metal-work, and dress. Most conspicuous of all were the locksmiths, joiners and cabinet-makers, shoemakers, and tailors; others frequently in evidence were stone-masons, hairdressers, and engravers; and, of those engaged in less skilful occupations, wine-merchants, water-carriers, porters, cooks, and domestic servants. Workers employed in manufactories (textiles, glass, tobacco, tapestries, porcelain) played, with the exception of the gauze-workers, a relatively inconspicuous role in these movements.

A study of these records confirms the traditional view that the parts of Paris most frequently and wholeheartedly engaged in the riots and insurrections of the Revolution were the Faubourgs Saint-Antoine and Saint-Marcel. This is strikingly borne out in the case of Saint-Antoine, whose craftsmen and journeymen initiated and dominated the Réveillon riots, the capture of the Bastille, and the overthrow of the monarchy, and played an outstanding part in the revolution of May–June 1793 and the popular revolt of Prairial; the police reports suggest, in fact, that it was only in the events of 1787– 8 and in the Champ de Mars affair that Saint-Antoine played little or no part. The Faubourg Saint-Marcel, on the other hand, while it contributed substantially to the commotions of September–October 1788 and was represented by a score of volunteers at the siege of the Bastille, only began to play a really conspicuous role in the spring and summer of 1791. After this the part it played was second only to that of Saint-Antoine in the revolutions of August 1792 and May–June 1793, and in the days of Prairial. In Vendémiaire, of course, the pattern was quite different. Although property-owners and "moderates" had by now taken charge of even the popular Sections, it was not they but the traditional *bourgeois* Sections of Lepeletier (Bibliothèque) and Butte des Moulins (Palais Royal) that took the lead and held the initiative, while—characteristically—it was the Quinze Vingts in the Faubourg Saint-Antoine which alone dispatched a contingent of armed volunteers to oppose the counter-revolutionary rebels.

But even if it can be demonstrated that the overwhelming majority of the participants in all but the last of the revolutionary *journées* were Parisian *sans-culottes,* how far can they be considered typical of the social groups from which they were drawn? Taine and his followers, while not denying the presence in revolutionary crowds of tradesmen, wage-earners, and city poor, insisted, nevertheless, that the dominant element among them were *vagabonds, criminels,* and *gens sans aveu.*[2] In view of the panic-fear engendered among large and small property-owners by vagrants, petty thieves, and unemployed at different stages of the Revolution, it is perhaps not surprising that such a charge should be made: it was certainly voiced on more than one occasion by hostile journalists, memorialists, and police authorities of the day. Yet, in its application to the capital at least, it has little foundation

in fact. Among the sixty-eight persons arrested, wounded, and killed in the Réveillon riots for whom details are available, there were only three without fixed abode—a cobbler, a carter, and a navvy. Of nearly eighty scheduled for arrest after the burning of the *barrières* and four arrested for breaking the windows of the Barrière Saint-Denis, all were of fixed abode and occupation. Of some sixty persons arrested at the time of the looting of the Saint-Lazare monastery in July 1789, nine were unemployed workers without fixed abode, who were caught up in the general drag-net directed against vagrants, *gens sans aveu,* and dwellers in lodging-houses at the time of the July revolution, and probably had no direct connexion with this affair at all. Every one of the 662 *vainqueurs de la Bastille* and of those claiming compensation for themselves and their dependents in August 1792 was of fixed abode and settled occupation. In the weeks preceding the Champ de Mars demonstration one beggar was arrested for abusing the king and queen, another for applauding their flight from Paris, and two more for causing a disturbance and insulting the National Guard; three other persons are described as being *sans état;* the rest of the 250 arrested during this period appear to have been of settled abode. Nor is there any mention in the records of vagrants or beggars among those arrested in Germinal and Prairial of the Year III; nor, even more surprisingly perhaps, among those implicated in the grocery riots of 1792 and 1793. Doubtless these elements mingled with the rioters and insurgents on such occasions, and we know that they caused concern to the Paris Electors during the revolution of July 1789; but they appear to have played an altogether minor role in these movements.

---

[2] Unemployed.—Ed.

This does not mean, of course, that unemployed workers or workers and craftsmen living in furnished rooms or lodginghouses (the often despised *non-domiciliés*) did not form a substantial element in revolutionary crowds. This was particularly the case in the early years of the Revolution, when, quite apart from the influx of workless countrymen, there was considerable unemployment in a large number of Parisian crafts; this, however, became a declining factor after the autumn of 1791. We find that eight of some fifty workers arrested or wounded in the Réveillon riots were unemployed and that the proportion was somewhat higher among those arrested in connexion with the Champ de Mars affair. In July 1789, too, there is circumstantial evidence to suggest that unemployed craftsmen, journeymen, and labourers (only a handful of whom were from *ateliers de charité*[3] were among those that took part in the assault on the Bastille: we know, for example, that substantial sums were raised after the fall of the fortress to relieve the distress of the *faubourg* and that, of 900 stone-cutters who later petitioned the Assembly for unemployment relief, several claimed to have been present at its capture. We have seen, too, that unemployed workers from neighbouring *ateliers de charité* played a certain part in the destruction of the *barrières* and the raid on the Saint-Lazare monastery. The *non-domiciliés* formed a substantial proportion of the wage-earners, small craftsmen, and petty traders of the capital, by no means limited to the unemployed or casual labourers, though it was a fiction of the time that the *hôtel* or *maison garnie*[4] provided only for provincials,

foreigners, cut-throats, thieves, and *gens sans aveu:* indeed, the *logeurs* or tenants of such premises were compelled by law to keep a daily check and to give a daily report to the police on all their lodgers. In view of their numbers it is hardly surprising to find them fairly well represented among those taking part in these disturbances—perhaps one in four of those arrested in the Réveillon affair, one in ten among the *vainqueurs de la Bastille,* one in five of those most actively concerned with the Champ de Mars movement, and one in six of those arrested and jailed in the grocery riots. But this is, of course, a quite separate question from that of Taine's *gens sans aveu* and gives no further indication of the number of vagrants involved.

The further contention that criminals and bandits played a significant part in the revolutionary *journées* collapses no less readily when looked at more closely. The police in crossexamining their prisoners habitually inquired whether they had served previous terms of imprisonment and it was easy enough to verify whether, as in the case of more serious offences, they had been branded with the notorious V of the thief or G of the galley-convict. The eight commissioners examining the Réveillon prisoners were able to find only three who had incurred previous convictions of any kind—in two cases these had involved short terms of detention in the Hôtel de la Force on minor charges, whereas the port-worker Téteigne was found to be branded with a V. Yet such a case is exceptional. Of those arrested for looting the Saint-Lazare monastery only one had served a prison sentence—the butcher's boy Quatrevaux, who had spent seventeen days in the Force on a previous conviction. Not one of the twenty-one arrested for the murder of Châtel, lieutenant to the mayor, during

[3] Charity hostel.—Ed.
[4] Rooming house.—Ed.

a food riot at Saint-Denis in August 1789, appears to have had a criminal record; and only three of fifteen arrested in a similar disturbance at Versailles in September had served previous sentences— one for stealing four pieces of wood in 1788 and two for minor breaches of army discipline. Of some 150 persons arrested in the Paris Sections for political offences during the months preceding and following the Champ de Mars affair, only four appear to have served previous sentences, and these, again, were of a trivial nature. Not one of the thirty-nine tried in the Year IV for alleged complicity in the September massacres had appeared in court before. Such information is, unfortunately, not available for the other great *journées* of the Revolution; yet this evidence, as far as it goes, is overwhelming and should prove conclusive. By and large it does not appear, in fact, that those taking part in revolutionary crowds were any more given to crime, or even to violence or disorder, than the ordinary run of Parisian citizens from whom they were recruited.

It may, of course, be argued that such persons were not fully typical of the Parisian *menu peuple* in so far as their participation in revolutionary events marks them off as a militant minority. This point should, however, not be pressed too far. It is presumably true enough of the small groups of *meneurs* . . . who probably played some part in even the most seemingly spontaneous of all these movements. . . . Again, the term may no doubt be used of those *sans-culottes*—rarely wage-earners, as we have seen—who played an active part in the Sections in the Year II, or were members of local Revolutionary Committees or even of the Commune: these are they of course to whom the epithet *sans-culotte*, in its sociopolitical sense, has most generally been applied. Doubtless, too, we should consider as a militant minority the recognized *vainqueurs de la Bastille*, those who stormed the Tuileries in August 1792, or who advanced on the Convention under arms in Prairial, and even those few hundred who denounced the Constituent Assembly and the National Guard in such downright, political terms—we have noted the case of the cook, Constance Évrard—in the spring and summer of 1791. Yet the term can hardly be applied with the same confidence to the labourers and journeymen who destroyed Réveillon's house, to the men and women who invaded grocers' shops and imposed their own, popular, form of price-control in 1792–3, to the many who applauded the September massacres (or even to the *massacreurs* themselves?), or to the women who marched to Versailles in October or who demonstrated for bread and the Constitution of 1793 in Prairial. Where, then, should we draw the line? This, of course, raises wider issues than those we have been considering in the present chapter. It may perhaps be possible to answer the question with greater assurance when we have examined the motives and other forms of compulsion that drew crowds together and released their revolutionary energies.

ALBERT SOBOUL (b. 1914), a leading French Marxist historian, has devoted much of his research to a detailed study of the Parisian masses. In this selection he describes the political organization, social composition, and economic objectives of the sans-culottes during the crisis years of 1793 and 1794.*

Albert Soboul

The Parisian Radicals

From June 1793 to February 1794, the Parisian sans-culotte movement played a major role in the political struggle leading to the consolidation of the Revolutionary Government and the organization of the Committee of Public Safety. During the same period, it imposed economic measures upon a reluctant Assembly intended to improve the living standards of the masses. If we wish to study the motives which explain the attitude of the people at this time, some kind of social definition of the Parisian sans-culotterie, some assessment of its composition is required.

This is not an easy task, for the economic or fiscal documents which could provide us with detailed analyses are missing, and what little statistical evidence we have is both vague and misleading. It is mainly through the political documents that we can explore the social characteristics of the sans-culotterie, particularly the dossiers dealing with the anti-terrorist repression of the Year III. The true image, the mentality and behaviour of the Parisian sans-culotte, only emerges by comparing the attitudes of two social groups. Not particularly conscious of class distinctions, the sans-culotte reveals himself most clearly in relation to his social enemies. This absence of class-consciousness is reflected in the social composition of the Parisian population—in so far as it is possible to analyse it—and even more strikingly in the

*Albert Soboul, *The Parisian Sans-Culottes and the French Revolution,* translated by G. Lewis (Oxford: Clarendon Press, 1964), pp. 18–54. Footnotes omitted.

social composition of the political personnel of the Sections.

If we attempt to delimit the social contours of the sans-culotterie, we should, first of all, discover how the sans-culotte defined himself. There are enough relevant documents available for us to make, at least, an approximate definition.

The sans-culotte was outwardly recognizable by his dress, which served to distinguish him from the more elevated classes of society. Trousers were the distinctive mark of the popular classes; breeches of the aristocracy, and generally speaking, of the higher ranks of the old Third Estate. Robespierre used to contrast the *culottes dorées* with the *sans-culottes* — those who wore fancy or embroidered breeches with those who simply wore trousers. The sans-culottes themselves made the same distinction. . . .

The sans-culottes readily judged a person's character from his appearance; his character then decided what his political opinions would be. Everyone who offended their sense of equality and fraternity was suspected of being an aristocrat. It was difficult for a former noble to find favour in their eyes, even when no definite accusation could be levelled against him. . . . "Their hearts are always full of pride, and we will never forget the air of superiority which they used to assume, nor the domination which they exercised over us." It was for these reasons that the *comité révolutionnaire* of the Section de la République arrested the duc de Brancas-Céreste on 16 October 1793, pointing out that he still enjoyed a yearly income of 89,980 *livres*. The sans-culottes could not endure pride or disdain, since these feelings were thought to be typically aristocratic and contrary to the spirit of fraternity which should reign amongst citizens equal in rights:

they obviously implied a political attitud hostile to the kind of democracy whic the sans-culottes practised in their genera assemblies and popular societies. . . .

On 17 September 1793, the committe of the Section Révolutionnaire decide to arrest Etienne Gide, a wholesale mer chant in watches and clocks, because h had given his allegiance to the Brissoti party, but also because he was of a "haught and proud" disposition, and had ofte been heard to speak "ironically." O 28 Brumaire, the committee of the Sectio des Marchés arrested a music-deale named Bayeux. It was alleged that h had said in a meeting of the general as sembly that "it was disgusting to see cobbler acting as president, particularl a cobbler who was so badly dressed." I the Section du Contrat-Social, the crim of the watchmaker Brasseur, who wa arrested on 23 Floréal, was his remar "that it was very disagreeable for a ma like himself to be in a guard-room wit the sort of people whom, in the old days one had nothing to do with." In extrem cases, a mere attitude of indifferenc towards a sans-culotte was enough for person to be charged with harbouring "aristocratic feelings." Explaining th arrest of a former banker, Girardot Marigny, on 12 Brumaire, the committe of the Section de Guillaume-Tell simpl observed that it was a case of "one of thes rich citizens who would not deign t fraternize with Republicans."

Even more incriminating in the eye of the sans-culottes than an attitude o pride, contempt, or plain indifference was an insinuation of their social inferiority. In its report of 9 Frimaire upon Louis-Claude Cezeron, arrested as a suspect, the committee of the Section Poissonnière referred in particular to some remarks he had made at a meeting of the general assembly in the preceding May, "that the poor depended upon the rich, and that the sans-culottes had never been anything but the lowest class of society." Bergeron, a dealer in skins from the Section des Lombards, "when he saw the sans-culottes fulfilling their obligations as citizens . . . said that it would be better if they got on with their own affairs instead of meddling in politics": he was arrested as a suspect on 18 Pluviôse. The sans-culottes also had no time for the type of person who took advantage of his social position, wealth, or even his education, to impress or influence those beneath him. Truchon, a lawyer from the Section de Gravilliers, who had been denounced on several occasions by Jacques Roux in his *Publiciste,* was finally arrested on 9 Prairial in the Year II: the *comité révolutionnaire* accused him of having influenced citizens of "little discernment," and of expressing the opinion that "positions of authority should be filled by enlightened men with private means, since they alone had the time to spare."

It is true that the sans-culottes had an egalitarian conception of social relationships. But beneath the general theory, there were more clearly defined factors which help to explain their behaviour, and it is interesting to consider to what extent they themselves were conscious of, and able to express, this deeper motivation.

Above all, the sans-culottes were conscious of the social antagonism which divided them from the aristocracy. The aristocracy had been the real enemy from 14 July 1789 to 10 August 1792, and it was against the aristocracy that they continued to struggle. . . .

The aristocrat was such a figure of hatred to the sans-culotterie that it was not long before the expression was being used to describe all their enemies, irrespective of whether they belonged to the former nobility or to the higher ranks of what had been the Third Estate. This failure to distinguish between the real aristocrat and a member of the upper bourgeoisie—which was peculiarly sans-culotte—helps to underline the separate and distinct character of their contribution to the Revolution.

On 25 July 1792, in an address demanding the dethronement of the king, the Section du Louvre denounced along with the landed aristocracy, "the ministerial, financial and bourgeois aristocracy, and, above all, the aristocracy of the refractory priests." By broadening its original meaning, the term "aristocrat" came to be used in the Year II to encompass every social group against which the sans-culottes were struggling. Hence the significant expression *aristocratie bourgeoise* which recurs so frequently in the texts, and the specifically popular definition given to it by an anonymous petitioner in the Year II, in which social and political considerations were intermingled. The "aristocrat" was the type of person who regretted the passing of the *ancien régime* and disapproved of the Revolution, did nothing to support it, and had not taken the civic oath, nor enlisted in the National Guard. He was the type of citizen who refused to buy National Lands, even though he had the opportunity and the means of doing so; he did not cultivate his lands, but refused to sell them at a reasonable price, or farm them out, or lease them on a system of *métayage.* The "aristocrat" did not find employment for labourers or journeymen, although he was very well able to do so; he did not contribute "at a rate relative to the cost of living" to the collections made for volunteers to the armies, and had done nothing to improve the conditions of poor and patriotic citizens. The "true patriot" was his opposite in every respect. The word "aristocrat," therefore, was used to describe all the enemies of the sans-culotterie—bourgeois as well as noble—who constituted "the class of citizens from whom we should levy the forced loan which must be raised throughout the Republic." Extreme sans-culottes no longer used the word "aristocrat" to designate the former nobility, but the bourgeoisie. On 21 May 1793, a popular orator from the Section du Mail stated that "aristocrats are the rich, wealthy merchants, monopolists, middlemen, bankers, trading clerks, quibbling lawyers and citizens who own anything."

The economic crisis helped to sharpen these social conflicts, and as the crisis developed and the *patriote* party of 1789 began to disintegrate, differences of opinion between the sans-culottes and the upper classes of the old Third Estate were added to the fundamental sans-culotte-aristocrat antagonism. . . . An address to the Convention on 27 Ventôse contrasts with the "brave sans-culottes," not only the clergy, the nobility and the sovereign heads of Europe, but also solicitors, barristers, notaries, and particularly "well-to-do farmers, selfish citizens and all these fat, wealthy merchants. They are fighting against us instead of our oppressors." Is this simply a struggle between citizens who owned property, and those who did not, a struggle between *possédants* and *non-possédants?* One cannot really say that it is, for we find craftsmen and shopkeepers amongst the sans-culotterie who were themselves property-owners. It is rather a conflict between those who favoured the idea of restricted and limited ownership, and those who believed in the absolute right of property as proclaimed in 1789; and even more clearly, a conflict between the defenders of a system of controls and

fixed prices, and those who preferred an economic policy of *laissez-faire*—in general terms, a struggle between consumers and producers.

The sources enable us to probe fairly deeply into the social antipathies and preoccupations of the sans-culotterie. They denounced *honnêtes gens*—those citizens who, if not rich, enjoyed at least a comfortable and cultured life, and also those who were conscious, if not necessarily proud, of being better dressed and better educated than themselves. They denounced *rentiers*—citizens who lived off unearned incomes. And finally they denounced "the rich"; not just property-owners or *possédants,* but the *gros* as opposed to the *petits*—the wealthy, big business-men as compared with those of their own kind who possessed but limited means. The sans-culottes were not hostile towards property so long as it was limited; they accepted property of the kind which artisans and shopkeepers already owned, and which many *compagnons* dreamed of owning themselves in the future. . . .

Thus, the instinctive reaction of the humblest citizen gradually became a systematic attitude of mind and, finally, a rule of political conduct amongst the more militant supporters of the Revolution. At the end of July 1793, when it looked as if the *possédants* were favouring the move towards federalism and forming the nucleus of the moderate party, a petition from the Section des Sans-Culottes demanded that the "aristocracy" be stripped of its wealth and reduced to beggary. A petition presented to the Convention by the Commune on 5 Frimaire called for the return of every wealthy citizen who had left Paris for the countryside, and denounced wealth as "a gangrene which corrupts everything which comes into contact with it, and everything which depends upon it." On

9 Ventôse, a member of the *commission des salpêtres* in the Section Chalier, discussing a report by the police-agent Charmont, assured his hearers "that he had never seen anything quite so grasping as the rich citizens of this Section." Whilst the poor were sacrificing more than they could afford, the rich thought twice about giving anything at all: "you have to hammer on the doors of these egoists who have no conception of what is meant by one's native-land."

This innate tendency amongst the sans-culotterie to attack the rich was encouraged in the Year II by leading political figures. . . . The actual social ideas of the Mountain and the Jacobins, their conception of class relationships, need not concern us here, nor do we need to question the sincerity of the Robespierrists; but it should be understood that this policy was only adopted as a tactical necessity, sometimes as a pretentious afterthought. The crisis from the spring to the autumn of 1793 made the popular alliance necessary: the sans-culottes represented the force which enabled the small section of the politically-conscious bourgeoisie to crush the aristocracy and its allies. "Internal dangers," wrote Robespierre in his notebook during the insurrection of 2 June, "come from the bourgeoisie. In order to overcome the bourgeoisie we have to rally the people." Some *représentants en mission*, such as Fouché in the department of the Nièvre, took stock of these necessities and resolutely carried out a social policy favourable to the popular classes.

The theme of hostility between the rich and the sans-culottes was obviously exploited for political reasons by those who did not share in the responsibilities of government—Jacques Roux at first, then Hébert composed several variations on it. The sans-culottes represented an important striking-force through which pressure could be brought to bear upon the various governmental committees, and there can be no doubt that Hébert and his colleagues were prepared to exploit it in order to attain their own particular objectives. . . . In its vulgar style, the *Père Duchesne* inveighed against the rich and exalted the poor: the expressions "the selfish rich," "the idle rich" and "the useless rich" are all to be found in its pages. Hébert was only giving expression to a general idea which the sans-culottes already possessed; but, through his vigorous style, he imprinted it more clearly upon their imagination, giving them a better appreciation of the nature of the class struggle, in which they were engaged.

Obviously, we should not overestimate the importance of this attitude. In defining the rich, the sans-culottes did not distinguish clearly between the aristocracy and the bourgeoisie; nor did they represent a composite social unit themselves, including as they did *compagnons*, craftsmen and shopkeepers. However, a few of the sans-culottes appeared to be conscious of a policy based upon class differences. On several occasions, they petitioned for, or tried to realize the disarmament of the rich. On 20 April 1793, a number of members of the Section du Contrat-Social proposed that the rich should be forced to return their weapons. . . . The most striking illustration of this attitude of mind was given in a petition from the Section de l'Observatoire on 29 September 1793 in which the "nation was contrasted with the wholesale-merchant class, bankers, speculators, and the rich in general. . . . Because the sans-culottes are, after all, much more numerous, and it should be clear to everyone that the nation is 'sans-culotte', and that the small number of people who dispose of its wealth cannot be the nation—they are only privileged citizens who are nearing the end of their privileges."

The more discerning members of the sans-culotterie began to realize that a privilege of wealth was taking the place of a privilege of birth. They foresaw that the bourgeoisie would succeed the fallen aristocracy as the ruling class. . . . However, it would be wrong to generalize about this frame of mind. It was impossible for the popular classes to gain a clear understanding of the social supremacy of the bourgeoisie until the aristocracy had finally been destroyed.

The hostile attitude of the sans-culotterie towards trade—one of the fundamental traits of popular mentality in the Year II—finally alienated sans-culotte sympathies for the rich. As urban consumers, the Parisian sans-culottes were naturally inclined to oppose those who controlled the supplies of basic commodities. As shopkeepers, they felt little affection for wholesalers. As craftsmen or *compagnons,* more rarely as workers in the real sense of the word, they remained small independent producers with no sympathy for, or understanding of, investors of commercial capital. The economic crisis and political struggles sharpened this antagonism inherent in the social position of the sans-culotterie. As food supplies grew scarce and the cost of living rose, every wholesale trader was soon suspected of being either a *monopoleur* or a hoarder. The struggle against the Girondins, then, after 31 May, against the moderates, was very often transformed into a struggle against the merchant bourgeoisie, at least in the Sections. The conflict became more acute as the sans-culottes continued to demand price fixing and controls on food supplies; as traders defended the freedom

of production and distribution, so they became objects of suspicion. A new social enemy was added to that of the landed and the religious aristocracy—the "merchant aristocracy." When, in the Year II, political power changed hands favouring the moderates, one of the grievances which was repeatedly made against former terrorists was that of having persecuted the merchants. . . .

In 1793 and in the Year III, sans-culotte hostility towards the merchants expressed itself during periods of acute crisis in violence and looting. It was also characterized by a constant desire for repression. . . .

Once popular power had been firmly established in the Sections, merchants quickly attracted the suspicions of the various *comités révolutionnaires* simply on account of their occupation. This attitude was encouraged by the Commune which, on 19 January, listed as suspects "those who sympathize with farmers and grasping merchants who must be made to feel the weight of the law." Some committees had not even waited for this encouragement. On 14 September, the Section des Lombards, where hostility against traders was particularly pronounced, had already placed a citizen named Dussautoy in custody, not only because of his indifference towards the Revolution, but because he was a grocer. The arrests of merchants went on until the spring of the Year II. . . .

It was not simply a question of arresting individuals: an entire social category came under fire; and although the sans-culottes rejected the idea of eliminating it completely from political life, they were agreed that it should be subjugated until it had been rendered harmless. On 3 October 1793, the general assembly of the Section de l'Unité asked that merchants "of whatever kind" should be excluded from the revolutionary tribunals. On 30 Nivôse Year II this same Section decided to name six *commissaires* to keep an eye on merchants "of all kinds." . . . the Commune, attacking the merchant aristocracy. Such attacks on trade and tradesmen were one of the favourite themes of the *Père Duchesne*. It was only after Hébert and Chaumette had been sentenced that the arrest of merchants came to an end and the denunciations of trade ceased. The Committee of Public Safety launched a new commercial policy, and the leaders of the Commune, having decided to end a campaign which threatened to undermine the traditional structure of society, began to reinstate a profession which was now considered to be indispensable to the war effort. . . .

For the militant or more extreme sans-culotte, it was a short step from hostility towards the merchants to a justification of pillage. Gillet, one of the most militant sans-culottes in the *société populaire des Quinze-Vingts* . . . incited workmen at the port de la Rapée to loot the property of the merchants, describing the latter as "swindlers and scoundrels." "The method he adopted to incite them to brigandage was to commiserate with their unfortunate lot, and to point out that they were earning too little. . . . " In a way, pillaging satisfied the deep-rooted egalitarian ideas of the sans-culottes . . . : individual acts of reprisals were justified by the inequalities in living conditions.

The profound antagonism which existed between the sans-culottes and the merchant bourgeoisie reveals itself more clearly in primitive impulses and terrorist exaltation than in the remarks made against traders or even in the encouragement given to pillaging. Many of the militant sans-culottes used the threat of the guillotine as an effective remedy against famine. In order to compel the farmers to sell their grain at a controlled price they demanded the creation of a revolutionary army, and once this had been decreed, they immediately began to ask for a mobile guillotine to accompany the army in order to make it more effective. . . .

It would appear from this that in order to gain a true picture of the sans-culotte it is necessary to depict him in opposition to the aristocracy, wealth, and commerce. The need for so negative an approach shows how vague the social boundaries within the old Third Estate were, and how difficult it is to define the sans-culotterie as a social class. The line of demarcation between the latter and the bourgeoisie was by no means clear. A coalition of disparate social elements, the unity of the sans-culotterie was undermined by internal contradictions. It is these contradictions which explain its incapacity to formulate a coherent policy and, in the last analysis, its political defeat

The ingrained hatred of the aristocracy was not confined to the sans-culottes alone. It had been shared in 1789 by practically every member of the Third Estate; although as the Revolution became more extreme, they began to reconsider their attitude, some sections of the bourgeoisie envisaging a compromise similar to that made in England during the Glorious Revolution of 1688. But in the Year II, the montagnard bourgeoisie—particularly its jacobin wing—remained resolutely at the head of the struggle against the aristocracy within France and on the frontiers. The demands of this struggle determined the entire policy of the Revolutionary Government.

Popular hostility against wealth and trade brought with it, on the other hand, certain contradictions, in as much as the sans-culotte shopkeeper and craftsman often owned his business premises. Their spokesmen were always careful to explain that their anger was directed simply against property-owning on a large scale. The violent outbursts in the *Père Duchesne* arose from the fact "that the *gros* continue to eat up the *petits.*" "Our native-land be damned! The merchants do not know what the word means," stormed Hébert, but then hastily added, "Do not let it be said that I despise trade. No one has more respect than I for the honest man who lives by his toil"— meaning the craftsman and small tradesman. Hébert did not suspect that the interests of the latter were not always identical with those of the *compagnon* or wage-earner. . . .

Fully aware of the fundamental antagonisms of *ancien régime* society, and consumed with hatred for the aristocracy —a hatred they shared with the montagnard bourgeoisie—the sans-culotterie were still not really "class-conscious." Divided into different social categories, sometimes with conflicting aims, it was practically impossible for them to constitute a class: their unity, in so far as it existed, was of a negative kind. One final point emphasizes this. According to popular mentality, a sans-culotte could not be defined by social characteristics alone: a counter-revolutionary workman could not be a good sans-culotte; a bourgeois patriot and republican might very well be accepted as one. The social definition must be qualified by a political definition: they cannot be separated. "One can only find virtue and patriotism," announces the *Père Duchesne,* "amongst sans-culottes: without them, the Revolution would be finished. The salvation of the Republic lies in their hands." Here the word sans-culotte is used as a synonym for patriot and republican.

For the sans-culotte, it was not simply a question of describing oneself as a sans-culotte, or of adopting a patronizing attitude towards the Revolution, it was a question of political conduct. The sans-culotte had taken part in the great revolutionary *journées;* he had fought for the democratic Republic. In the general assembly of the Section des Marchés on 9 Prairial Year III, Hébert, an itinerant herbalist and a sans-culotte, defended himself against charges of terrorism by reminding his accusers of his services to the Republic: "Of course I am a terrorist," he admitted, "but the only proof I have given of it is before the château of the tyrant Capet on 10 August, when my terrorism cost me my right arm. . . . " A still more precise definition was given by Brutus Magnier, president of a military commission to the *armées de l'Ouest* in the Year II. Having criticized "the government which has sworn the downfall of the sans-culottes" in a letter seized by the authorities, he was asked during his interrogation on 21 Messidor Year III what he meant by the word sans-culotte. Magnier replied: "I would say that it meant the conquerors of the Bastille, the victors of the '10 August' and the '31 May', particularly the latter who appear to have had an eternal war sworn against them. It also refers to those who had been described as terrorists and *buveurs de sang* by those cannibals who more justly deserve these titles." The sans-culotte, therefore, is defined by his political behaviour as much as by his place in society—the latter is more difficult to ascertain than the former.

A document dated May 1793 attempts to answer part of this difficulty, at least, in replying to "the impertinent question—what is a sans-culotte?" The sans-culotte " . . . is someone who goes everywhere on foot . . . and who lives quite simply with his wife and children, if he has any, on the fourth or fifth floor." Jacques Roux also referred to the sans-culottes living in attics, and the *Père Duchesne* wrote, "If you wish to meet the cream of the sans-culotterie, then visit the garrets of the workers (ouvriers)." The sans-culotte is useful "because he knows how to plough a field, how to forge, to saw, to file, to cover a roof and how to make shoes. . . . And since he works, it is certain that you will not find him at the café de Chartres, ... In the evening, he goes to his Section, not powdered and perfumed, not elegantly dressed in the hope of catching the eye of the citizens in the galleries, but to give his unreserved support to sound resolutions. . . . Besides this, the sans-culotte always has his sword with the edge sharpened to give a salutary lesson to all trouble-makers. Sometimes he carries his pike with him, and at the first beat of the drum, he will be seen leaving for the Vendée, for the *armée des Alpes* or the *armée du Nord*."

The modest social condition of the sans-culotte is clearly of importance here; but, as we can see from the above document, a definition of the sans-culotte would not be complete without a statement of his political conduct.

If we attempt a statistical analysis of the Parisian Sections in the Year II on the basis of the texts and political documents at our disposal, we are confronted with the same difficulties when it comes to defining the sans-culotterie, and of establishing its proportion to the population of Paris as a whole.

To begin with it is impossible to say precisely what the population of Paris was at this time: it is even more difficult to estimate the proportion of the sans-culotterie in each Section. The law of 11 August 1793 ordered a census to be taken of the population of each Section, but although this began in the Year II it proceeded very slowly. Only ten Sections had been completed by Thermidor, and the census dragged on through the Year III. On 11 Fructidor, the *Comité de division* decided to draw up a list of all the holders of bread cards registered in the Sections. Its *Tableau Sommaire* of the population of Paris gives us a total of 640,504 inhabitants: a figure greater than the census taken at the time of the States General in 1789, and one which is doubtless exaggerated—the Sections being anxious to produce a list with a greater number of mouths to feed than they actually had. However, it does agree roughly with a statement of the population of Paris *relativement aux subsistances* of 13 Pluviôse Year III which appears to have escaped notice until now, and which gives a figure of 636,772 inhabitants.

However approximate these figures may be, they do throw an interesting light upon the pressure which the population in the various Sections exercised on the problem of food supplies. The Section du Panthéon-Francais was the most densely populated with 24,977 inhabitants, followed very closely by the Gravilliers Section with 24,774. On the other hand, it is remarkable that the Sections in the *faubourgs* of Saint-Antoine and Saint-Marcel were not amongst the most populated zones. In the former, the Section des Quinze-Vingts reached fifth place with 18,283 inhabitants, but Montreuil was only seventeenth (13,478), and Popincourt thirty-sixth (10,933). The Section du Finistère in the *faubourg* Saint-Marcel was listed as thirtieth with 11,775 inhabitants. Two thickly populated areas appear in the heart of Paris on either side of the Seine. On the right bank there were 180,000 people living in the twelve Sections of the centre; on the left bank, the four Sections of Unité, Bonnet-Rouge, Mutius-Scaevola, and Marat included over 70,000 inhabitants. In the Year II, these different Sections were amongst the most politically active in Paris—the shortage of food supplies being felt more acutely there than anywhere else. . . .

On the fringe of the working population, exercising a decisive influence on the population of Paris as a whole during times of scarcity, stood thousands of wretched and starving human beings. According to a report presented to the General Council of the Commune by the hospital administrator Danjou on 14 Germinal Year II, the number of destitute persons *(indigents secourus)* who had been given assistance in all the Sections of Paris reached a total of 68,981, or, if we use the population returns *relativement aux subsistances* of Pluviôse Year III, about one person in every nine obtained relief from the authorities in Paris. The pressure exerted by these unfortunate people varied from Section to Section. It was particularly strong in the historic *faubourgs,* throwing light upon their political activity during the Revolution. . . .

From these figures, we can build a social picture of the Parisian sans-culotterie which emphasizes the essential feature of popular movements during the Revolution—that of hunger.

If in times of crisis, the complex and solid mass of the Parisian sans-culotterie provided the impetus behind the more violent episodes in the Revolution, in calmer times, less worried about the provision of its food, it paid only a fluctuating attention to political affairs. Not every sans-culotte was a militant. A study of the sectionary political personnel in the Year II will give us a more complete and more balanced social description of the Parisian sans-culotterie.

For this study, the most important material has been taken from the collection of dossiers forming the alphabetical series of papers of the Committee of General Security. Based primarily on the repression of Prairial Year III, in some respects they throw as much light on the Thermidorean psychology of the property-owning classes as on the terrorist mentality of the sans-culottes themselves. We need, therefore, to be very careful about accepting the many denunciations contained in these documents. . . . The numerous files dealing with disarmament and arrests present an equally valuable documentation, the only one which gives us direct information on the political personnel of the Sections as a whole.

The nature of this evidence does not, by any means, enable us to make an exact statistical study—the age of the militant sans-culottes is rarely indicated; their profession is often omitted; the vocabulary is loose and misleading. Any study of the social composition of the sans-culotterie is, therefore, beset by many uncertainties. At the end of the eighteenth century, manual workers were frequently referred to, rather disdainfully, as *le peuple* by the propertied-classes, aristocrats and the bourgeoisie. The bookseller Hardy writing in his *Journal* unites under the same phase—*menu peuple*— the non-propertied-classes and the lower middle class Parisians who were, in fact, often property-owners—small tradesmen and workshop masters as well as *compagnons,* labourers and the destitute. In fact, there are as many shades of difference between the lower middle-classes and the proletariat as there are varieties of social conflict. . . . The head of a business concern kept his professional qualification and still described himself as a "cabinet-maker" or a "carpenter" even when he was employing dozens of workers. This was the case with the "fan-maker" Mauvage, a militant sans-culotte in the Section du Faubourg-du-Nord: we have to study his dossier carefully before we discover that he owned a factory which employed sixty people. The same word is used to describe social realities which are basically different, and we have to decide in each case exactly where these artisans and shopkeepers belonged in the social hierarchy. At what point does the work of a craftsman become a business concern? More often than not, the documents of the period fail to distinguish between the *compagnon,* the small craftsman and the contractor: the degrees of difference between them are multiple, and the transition from one to the other is graded into many stages. Any attempt to fix a rigid system of classification upon so fluid a society must be arbitrary. In any case, it would not be possible to make a really satisfactory study if we were to rely solely on the political documents: we need to determine the financial resources of the militants. However, the absence of fiscal documents for the Parisian Sections makes this extremely difficult. Intensive research into the notarial records might perhaps compensate for this loss, at least for those sans-culottes whose social standing bordered on the edge of the middle bourgeoisie. As for the records dealing with the lowest strata of Parisian society, they have disappeared altogether unless reference to them can be found in the dossiers of the anti-terrorist repression.

The political personnel of the Parisian Sections in the Year II may be divided, according to their functions and their social background, into three categories illustrating the social diversity of the sans-culotterie. The personnel of the *comités civils* represented the oldest, most stable and most prosperous category, and were often considered as belonging to the middle bourgeoisie. A later institution, the *comités révolutionnaires* were more popular in origin. The personnel of these committees were very soon paid for their services. From March 1793 to Fructidor Year II, they suffered from the repercussions of political upheavals, becoming more and more democratic until the autumn of 1793. The third category was that of the ordinary militant sans-culottes, mostly to be found after the autumn in the *sociétées sectionnaires,* representing the most popular elements of the sans-culotterie.

Created by the municipal law of 21 May –27 June 1790, and composed of citizens with the necessary qualifications for voting, the *comités civils* were largely renewed after 10 August 1792. Most of the *commissaires* on these committees kept their posts from this date to the Year III, some of them even escaping the reprisals in Prairial. Their purely administrative function provided them with the opportunity to stand aloof from political terrorist activities. Moreover, although the committees received money from the municipality for their expenses, the *commissaires* were for a long time unpaid. It was only on 6 Floréal Year II that the Convention voted the payment of three *livres* a day in recognition of their public services. This allowance came too late for the personnel of these committees to be democratized. The *commissaires civils* belonged mostly to the higher ranks of the sans-culotterie. The money which they earned from their workshops, or from their business interests, permitted them to devote their time to their administrative tasks.

The *comité révolutionnaires,* at first paid only their expenses, but later salaried, were more democratically recruited than the *comités civils.* They represented the more popular elements of the sans-culotterie. Few of the *commissaires* lived off their own incomes— only 20, or 4.6 per cent. of the total number of 454; whereas 26.2 per cent. of the members of the *comités civils* did so. Amongst them only 4 were *rentiers* in the full sense of the word (0.8 per cent.); 11 belonged to the liberal professions (2.4 per cent.), and 6 were former shopkeepers or artisans (1.3 per cent.). Although there were few heads of business concerns, there were also no really popular elements. Manufacturers, contractors, or master-craftsmen accounted for 13 (2.8 per cent. as compared with 2.3 per cent. for the *comités civils*). On the other hand, we find 22 wage-earners, operatives, *compagnons* or apprentices, and 23 domestic servants or former domestic servants— a total of 9.9 per cent. The liberal professions were represented by 52 *commissaires*—artists, sculptors, painters, musicians, and schoolteachers: lawyers were relatively few. To this group we can add 22 lower-grade civil servants *(employés),* 7 of whom were employed by the Post Office (4.8 per cent.).

Here again, most of the *commissaires* were craftsmen or shopkeepers: 290 out of the total of 454, or 63.8 per cent. of the personnel of the *comités révolutionnaires.* Altogether, 206 *commissaires* (45.3 per cent.) could be considered as having some connexion with the artisan class; 84 were engaged in commerce (18.5 per cent.). The craftsmen are relatively more numerous than in the *comités civils:* for many of them, expenses of three, and later of five *livres* a day, compensated for

the decline or total loss of their trade: this is substantiated by the number of craftsmen connected with the luxury or art trades. The 28 shoemakers form the most important group (6.1 per cent.), followed by the 18 cabinet-makers (3.9 per cent.), then 16 wig-makers or hairdressers (3.5 per cent.). But there were 42 *commissaires* connected with some branch or other of the art trade (9.2 per cent.). A group of 37 *commissaires* were builders (8.1 per cent.), and 29 were timber-merchants or furniture-makers (6.3 per cent.).

Amongst the 84 persons engaged in trade, 41 described as merchants appear to have held a status above that of an ordinary shopkeeper. Ten wine merchants, whether wholesale or retail traders, headed the list, to which we can add six who sold soft drinks. The sale of drinks played an important part in the political life of the Sections. Another 15 dealt in the provision of food supplies: there were 6 grocers, 3 pastry-cooks, a baker, a fruiterer, also 2 restaurant-owners and 2 inn-keepers.

Scattered hints in individual dossiers sometimes enable us to discover the social standing of these *commissaires.* Many craftsmen and shopkeepers who had been more or less ruined by the loss of customers found a means of livelihood in the salaried duties of a *commissaire.* This explains the large numbers of wig-makers, hairdressers and shoemakers to be found on the *comités révolutionnaires,* as well as the domestic servants who had lost their positions, particularly numerous in the committee of the Section du Bonnet-Rouge in what used to be the *faubourg* Saint-Germain. . . .

If many of the *commissaires* found that their duties rewarded them with an income which they could no longer derive from their occupations, some on the other hand, still enjoyed either a modest income or a situation of some importance. Lambert, a *commissaire* in the Section de l'Arsenal, was a former domestic servant living on his small private income. Etienne Fournier, *commissaire* for the Section de l'Indivisibilité who had been a crockery-dealer, enjoyed an income of 1,700 *livres,* the yearly salary of an ordinary *employé.* . . . The dyer Barrucand from the Section de l'Arsenal, "conqueror of the Bastille," a *commissaire* dealing with the manufacture of pikes, member of the *comité révolutionnaire,* admitted that he was worth 21,600 *livres.* . . .

Other *commissaires* were important business men. In the Section des Gardes-Françaises, Maron, a plaster-manufacturer, employed twenty workmen in the quarry which he owned. As for Mauvage, *commissaire* in the Section du Faubourg-du-Nord, a really militant sans-culotte, we have seen that he was responsible for a fan-making concern employing sixty workers: nevertheless, he still called himself a "fan-maker." Some profited from their circumstances to put themselves on their feet financially and to rise in the social scale. Candolle, *commissaire* in the Section de l'Arsenal, previously a porter, became a wine-merchant. Larue, a member of the *comité révolutionnaire* of the Section des Lombards, did even better—an apprentice mason in 1789, he had become a building-contractor by the Year II. According to those who informed against him in the following year, "The Commune had given him work on various projects which helped him to make his money."

Although the *comités révolutionnaires* drew more upon the popular classes than the *comités civils,* they still reveal very much the same social pattern—from wage-earner to the large employer. The sans-culotterie did, indeed, represent a coalition of socially heterogeneous elements.

If we look at the third category of the political personnel in the Sections in the Year II—that of the militants, we arrive at the same conclusion, with the slight difference, however, that the wage-earning element in this group is more important. Out of the total number of 514 militants counted (and by the word "militant" we mean every citizen who played an active political role, whether in the popular society or in the general assembly, and who, for this reason, became a victim of the reaction of the Year III), 64 were wage-earners—*compagnons,* operatives, apprentices, journeymen or day-labourers—a percentage of 12.4. If we add to this list domestic servants, odd-job men, office-boys and shop-assistants, 40 in all (7.7 per cent.), the popular element forms 20.1 per cent. of the militant group, as opposed to 9.9 per cent. of the personnel of the *comités révolutionnaires,* and 0.8 per cent. of the *comités civils.* As a contrast, we find only one *rentier* and one landlord, 8 shopkeepers or retired traders (1.9 per cent.), whereas on the *comités révolutionnaires* and *comités civils* this group represented 4.6 per cent. and 26.2 per cent. respectively. The number of contractors or manufacturers is also quite small—only 4, or 0.7. On the *comités civils,* this percentage rises to 2.3 per cent. and to 2.8 per cent. on the *comités révolutionnaires.* As for the liberal professions, they are represented by 35 militants (6.8 per cent.), to which we can add 45 *employés,* making a total percentage 15.5. This group of *employés* is particularly important for, more often than not, they formed the life-blood of the *sociétés sectionnaires.*

The shopkeeper and, above all, the artisan class predominate amongst the militants, although the proportion is lower than for either of the two committees—81 tradesmen (15.7 per cent.), and 214 craftsmen, (41.6 per cent.). Amongst the tradesmen, 34 (6.6 per cent.) are described as merchants. The 18 engaged in the grocery trade were the most numerous, but the 10 wine-merchants are placed on top of the list, confirming the importance of their contribution to the political life of the Sections.

Amongst the 214 artisans, the shoemakers form a compact group of 41 militants (7.9 per cent. of the whole), followed by 24 hairdressers and wig-makers, and 20 tailors: should we, perhaps, establish a relationship between the militant activity of these small craftsmen and their professional difficulties? The building trade accounts for 30 militants (5.8 per cent.), there were 29 engaged in the timber and furniture trades (5.6 per cent.), but only 23 from the art and luxury trades (4.4 per cent.). Thus the trades which demanded fewer professional qualifications provided a large number of militants. For the *comités civils* and *comités révolutionnaires* the proportion was reversed: the artisans were really an *élite* to which the sans-culottes in many of the Sections looked for leadership.

Although the wage-earning element predominated amongst the militants, there were also many citizens who were comfortably situated, financially and socially. In the Section des Droits-de-l'Homme, Varlet possessed an income of 5,800 *livres*. In addition to his salary as a postal clerk, this *enragé* had a small income of his own, and could obviously be regarded as a representative of the middle classes. François Mercier in the Section Marat, formerly an assistant in a hat shop, was a juror on the Revolutionary Tribunal. He had invested the 12,150 *livres* which he had inherited from his mother in 1780 in a life insurance policy.

He said that he had taken an interest "in the business affairs of different people," and had also saved from his income, and from his fees as a juror, the sum of 9,430 *livres*. In the Year III, he stated that he was worth 21,580 *livres*. Bouland, an active militant from the *société de Lazowski* and the Section du Finistère, who never stopped "condemning the activities of merchants," had bought a house at the beginning of the Revolution in the boulevard Hôpital. Damoye, a saddle-merchant in the Section de Montreuil was arrested in Pluviôse Year III for his terrorist activities in the previous year. In his defence statement, he described himself as a well-to-do property-owner, adding that "he has his living to think of, and, for this reason, has suffered great anxiety since he was put under arrest two months ago." In the Year IV, the same man was asked for a forced loan of 3,000 *livres* (hard currency). Damoye was a typical example of the bourgeois sans-culotte.

Thus, if we analyse the composition of the political personnel of the Sections in the Year II, as well as the part played by the *faubourg* Saint-Antoine and to a lesser extent by the *faubourg* Saint-Marcel in the revolutionary movement and the important *journées* from July 1789 to Prairial Year III, we must conclude that the revolutionary *avant-garde* of the Parisian sans-culotterie did not constitute an industrial proletariat, but a coalition of small master-craftsmen and *compagnons* who worked and lived with them. This explains certain characteristics of the popular movement, as well as certain contradictions, arising from the ambiguous situation in which the sans-culottes often found themselves.

The small master-craftsman, working and living with his *compagnons*, very often a former *compagnon* himself, exercised a decisive ideological influence on the latter. Through him, bourgeois influences penetrated into the world of the workman. Even if he was in conflict with him, the small workshop *compagnon* inevitably derived many of his ideas from his employer, and often living and eating under the same roof had basically the same attitude to the great problems of the day. It was the lower middle-class craftsman who fashioned the mentality of the worker. However, having said this, many small problems remain to be solved. In particular, we must distinguish between the "independent" craftsman of Paris and the "dependent" craftsman, the classic example of the latter being the silk-weavers of Lyons —*le canut lyonnais.* Juridically free and head of his concern, possessing his own machine, even in a position to hire his own labour, the latter has all the appearance of an employer. But economically he is only a wage-earner, strictly dependent upon the merchant who supplies him with the raw material and who distributes the finished article. The interests of the "dependent" craftsman and the *compagnon* are the same—confronted with merchant capitalism they demanded price-controls and a basic minimum wage. But they did not go so far as to work out a direct relationship between the nature of the work and the rate of pay: wages were determined by the cost of living, not by the value of the work done. The social function of labour is not clearly understood. The dependent craftsman stands in an intermediate position between the *compagnon* and the independent craftsman aspiring towards the status of a lower middle-class citizen.

As for the wage-earning worker in the large manufacturing concerns, more important in the centre of Paris between the Seine and the *barrières,* less widespread in the *faubourgs,* they sometimes showed a more independent spirit which, to some extent, foreshadowed that of the proletariat of the great modern industrail concerns: the Réveillon affair, which turned into a riot on 28 April 1789, was a case in point. But more often than not the wage-earners in these larger manufacturing ventures had begun employment in small workshops. The spirit of the craftsman which they retained was strengthened by the environment in which they lived—a small minority of factory-workers surrounded by far greater numbers of *compagnons.* Labour as a whole carried the imprint of lower middle-class artisan mentality, and like it, the Parisian labour-force shared its bourgeois ideology. Neither in thought, nor deed, could the Parisian workman become an independent element during the Revolution.

There was a serious contradiction in this situation which affected the sans-culotte's attitude to his work, his position in society and his political activity. Although they shared their mode of living with their *compagnons,* craftsmen still owned their workshops, their equipment, and looked upon themselves as independent producers. The fact that they exercised authority over *compagnons* and apprentices accentuated their bourgeois mentality. Nevertheless the system of small production and direct sale was diametrically opposed to the ideas of the merchant bourgeoisie and commerical capitalism. In consequence, these craftsmen and shopkeepers who formed the more articulate section of the sans-culotterie cherished a social ideal which was incompatible with the evolution of the economic system. They campaigned against the concentration of the means of production, but they were themselves property-owners. When the more extreme sans-culottes demanded a maximum of wealth in the Year II, the contradiction between their own social position and this demand escaped them. They expressed their feelings in passionate outcries and bursts of revolt, but never in a coherent programme. The same was true of the individuals and political groups which shared their outlook—Jacques Roux, Hébert, even Robespierre and Saint-Just.

Failing to define their place in society as a working population, the sans-culottes had no clear and precise idea of the nature of labour itself. They did not appreciate that it had a social function of its own; they only considered it in relation to property. The bourgeoisie in a century of enlightment had restored the arts and crafts to their rightful place, they had given an incomparable impetus to the forces of invention; but, concentrating their attention mainly upon the problems of technique and production, they had not conceived of the idea of labour as part of the social structure. From 1789 to 1794, the bourgeoisie had never thought about labour problems in themselves or in relation to the workers, but always with regard to the interests of their own class: the Le Chapelier law is evidence of this. If the Convention decreed the General Maximum on 29 September 1793 after constant pressure from the sans-culotterie, it was, as far as the montagnard bourgeoisie were concerned, simply a tactical move. Price-controls were related essentially to food supplies; salaries were not in any way determined by the amount of work a man performed. Divided between a predominantly artisan economy and nascent industrialism, lacking all sense of class-consciousness, how could the Parisian labour-force fail to be influenced by the bourgeoisie into

whose hands it had largely entrusted th defence of its interests in the vital strug gle against the aristocracy: its attitud to the problems of labour could onl reflect prevailing political and socia conditions. For the bourgeoisie, propert was the key to the problem. The Declara tion of 1793, like that of 1789, had estab lished it as the first of the imprescriptibl Rights of Man, after the abolition o feudalism had made it an absolute right For the sans-culottes in the Year II, th problem of labour was not their primar social preoccupation. They were far to aware of their interests as consumers— it was not the question of strike-actio or demands for higher wages whic roused the sans-culotterie, but the ques tion of food supplies. A rise or fall in th cost of the main products of popular con sumption, grain and, above all, bread which accounted for at least half of th family expenditure, was the decisive factor which tightened or eased the wage earner's budget. The sans-culottes looked for a fixed system of price-controls on basic commodities; the demand for a sliding-scale of prices was exceptional. This perspective reflects economic and social conditions, as well as the ideology of the period.

Price-controls on basic commodities were demanded with all the more insistence by the militants because they were subjected to pressure in their respective Sections, not only from wage-earners, but also from the thousands of destitute Parisians, tormented by hunger. Hunger—an essential factor in all popular movements—was the cement which held together the artisan, the shopkeeper, and the workman, just as a common interest united them against the wealthy merchant, the contractor, the noble, and the bourgeois monopolist. From a sociological point of view, the erm "sans-culotte" may appear to be vague, but from the standpoint of the social conditions of the time, it reflects reality. It is true that the political moves explaining popular behaviour must not be excluded—particularly hatred of the nobility, the belief in the "aristocratic plot," the desire to destroy privilege and to establish equality before the law. How else can we account for the enthusiasm and disinterestedness of the sans-culotte volunteers? But the riots of February 1793, like the popular movement of the following summer, do not entirely fit into the general pattern of the bourgeois revolution: to quote Robespierre himself, these events were due to the popular demand for cheap and shoddy goods. The aim of the maximum, so stubbornly insisted upon and finally imposed on 29 September 1793, was to provide the wage-earners with their daily bread, not to facilitate the problems of national defence: the permanent motive behind popular action is to be found in the hardship of everyday life. In the last analysis, it can be said that economic fluctuations provided the rhythm of the revolutionary movement.

On 1 Prairial Year III, the tailor Jacob Clique from the Section des Gardes-Françaises was arrested for having said: "One would think that the buyers and the farmers are plotting together to sell everything as dearly as possible in order to starve the workman." Questioned about this statement, he replied: "I am embittered by misfortune. The father of three young children, without any resources, my daily work has to provide a living for five people. I was given hardly any work throughout the difficult winter we have just faced." Political demands were linked in a confused way with the demand for bread. "Under Robespierre," the cabinet-maker Richer from the Section de la République was alleged to have said on 1 Prairial, "blood flowed and there was enough bread to go round. Today, blood no longer flows and there is a shortage of it. It seems, therefore, that we must spill a little blood before we can get bread." The sans-culottes could not forget that during the Terror, despite every difficulty, there was no shortage. The political behaviour of the terrorist is intimately linked with the demand for bread, and it was this dual factor which cemented the unity of the Parisian sans-culotterie.

The rebellion in the Vendée is the subject of the research by CHARLES TILLY (b. 1929). He has recently completed a major book on the Vendean counterrevolution. In this selection drawn from an article he wrote while at the University of Delaware, Tilly employs sociological techniques to clarify the conditions which produced the uprising.*

Charles Tilly

A Counterrevolutionary Revolt

Through a species of dialectic, counterrevolutions often reveal the character of the revolutions against which they are directed. Resistance to a revolution may show, more clearly than its apparently unanimous acceptance, which elements of the population are the revolution's propelling force. For this reason, the Vendée, the massive revolt which broke out in the west of France in 1793, is of particular interest to those who wish to understand the French Revolution. . . .

Yet much of the traditional history of the Vendée is of little help in understanding the Revolution. Let us leave aside the dramatic military history of the counterrevolution, over which there is not much dispute, and the questions of

hagiography, which so easily trip up the wanderer among so many heroes and exploits. These matters, although they probably fill nine-tenths of the mountain of books written on the Vendée, are not very important for the general history of the Revolution. That leaves the perplexing problem of the origins and development of the counterrevolution. Those historians who have faced this problem seriously are a mere handful in the throng who have written accounts of the Vendée, but even they have not found a satisfying solution. . . .

There are three problems that ought to attract our attention: the distinguishing characteristics of those sections of the west in which the counterrevolution

---

*Charles Tilly, "Some Problems in the History of the Vendée," in *American Historical Review*, LXVII, no. 1 (1961), pp. 19–33. Footnotes omitted.

flourished; the formation and composition of the two competing parties, revolutionary and counterrevolutionary; the relationship between developments before 1793 and the outbreak of the rebellion. It may be wise to begin by explaining why these problems are important, and why they are difficult. . . .

The counterrevolution was a creature of the *bocage,* the granite-based mass of land south of the Loire, which is settled in relatively dispersed hamlets and isolated farms and is covered with small fields surrounded by high hedgerows. The Revolution was generally successful in the areas of river valley and plain, with their concentrated settlements and open fields. This observation in itself is commonplace. What is important is that the differences in habitat were accompanied by differences in the positions of the major social classes.

The *bocage* enclosed a considerable number of nobles, frequently resident, who owned most of the land exploited by the peasants, while in valley and plain the nobles were much more frequently weak and absent. The peasants of the *bocage* were mainly subsistence farmers, living on medium-sized rented or sharecropped family farms, selling enough cattle to cover rents, taxes, and little more. The principal intermediary between peasant community and outside world was the curé.

Valley and plain included large ecclesiastical properties as well as considerable bourgeois and peasant holdings, often extremely fractionated. Along the Loire the rich lands of such abbeys as Fontevrault and St. Florent often adjoined the plots of *bécheurs* and *laboureurs à bras*—peasants with holdings small and fruitful enough to be worked profitably by a man with a spade and his own two

arms, instead of by a great team of six, eight, or even ten oxen, as in the *bocage.* The crops of these areas were often specialized and destined for urban markets: wine, wheat, flax, hemp. Their producers included a much larger proportion of day laborers and of owners of small pieces of land than in the *bocage.* This summarizes the agricultural complex.

There was also an industrial complex, and the surprising fact is that industry was more developed in the *bocage,* at least in those sections that joined most actively in the counterrevolution. By far the most important was the textile industry, called the manufacture of Cholet, but actually scattered among more than ten thousand looms in a wide territory around that city. In the perspective of France as a whole, or even of the west, the manufacture of Cholet was of secondary importance. In the area of the rebellion there was, nevertheless, a growing class of merchants and clothiers, and in a great many communes weavers comprised 20 per cent of the working population. The features of this domestic production of kerchiefs and colored cloth that make it interesting for the present discussion are that it drew much of its raw material from outside the *bocage,* particularly from the Loire Valley, and that it placed its finished products on a national and world market, particularly via the port of Nantes. This means that in the *bocage* there was a small but prospering group of merchants who had relatively little to do with the local peasants, but much to do with both the local weavers and their colleagues outside the *bocage.* It also means that the cities, small as they were, were devoted to a commerce that drew their interests far outside the region.

This rapid summary indicates the essentials of the contrast: the plain and valley, combining peasant proprietors and day laborers who produced for outside markets, a relatively strong bourgeoisie, and extensive ecclesiastical properties; the *bocage,* populated with subsistence farmers dependent on noble landlords, a parish clergy with a strong hand in local affairs, a growing semirural proletariat attached to the textile industry, and a small but rising mercantile bourgeoisie. These facts alone would probably permit us to predict that the bourgeois would have an easier time developing a following and encouraging support for the Revolution in the first set of areas, and would meet greater resistance from nobles and clergy and receive less support from the rest of the population in the *bocage.*

It is essential to notice that the contrast between the two sections of the west, "blue" and "white," revolutionary and counterrevolutionary, existed long before the Revolution and persisted long after it. Religious practice and political preference have followed the same frontiers well into the twentieth century. An adequate analysis of the counterrevolution must therefore provide an understanding both of the temporary circumstances that agitated the west in 1793 and of the enduring characteristics of those sections that joined the rebellion.

The parties of *patriotes* and *aristocrates* formed early in the Revolution, although it is not yet clear how widespread identification with one or the other was before the first applications of the Civil Constitution of the Clergy and the first sales of Church property, both early in 1791. These constituted the first deep thrusts of the Revolution into the heart of the countryside and were, therefore, the first occasions on which many countrymen had to declare their positions publicly. From that time on, what there was of a third party was inexorably ground to dust between the turning stones of revolution and counterrevolution.

The great majority of the clergy, particularly the secular clergy, belonged to the counterrevolutionary party. This may seem quite normal, until we recognize that it set off the *bocage* distinctly from the surrounding area. The most convenient indication is the oath aligning the clergy with the Civil Constitution, generally administered at the beginning of 1791. In the districts where the rebellion arose, the proportion of the clergy taking the oath was under 15 per cent, while in the surrounding "patriot" districts, it was generally well over 50 per cent. In fact, the constitutional clergy who were brought in to replace those who had refused the oath were commonly curates and monks from the districts outside the *bocage.*

Nobles of the region were even more uniformly opposed to the Revolution. Despite the common supposition that the nobles agitated and even organized the rebellion, however, they were very little in evidence in the party conflicts of 1791 and 1792. A number of the great nobles who were to be counterrevolutionary chiefs, such as Henri de la Rochejaquelein and Artus de Bonchamp, were with the King until late in 1792, many more nobles had emigrated long before the counterrevolution, and the rest had retired to their châteaux without meddling much in local affairs.

According to the paradoxical terminology of the time, the bulk of the peasants of the *bocage* were "aristocrats," opponents of the Revolution. Here again is a remarkable contrast with the surrounding territories, where the peasants formed revolutionary clubs, bought Church properties, and gave all the other usual signs of support for the Revolution.

The bourgeois, particularly merchants, clothiers, and others involved in commerce and industry, were the heart of the patriots. In southern Anjou, we find *négociants*[1] and *marchands* everywhere in the lists of local officeholders and of purchasers of Church properties on the counterrevolutionary side of the line, while in the patriot country near Saumur, we find rather more lawyers, administrators, and substantial farmers. In many parts of the *bocage* the few bourgeois were the only adherents of the Revolution.

Artisans are at once the most troublesome and the most interesting category. The auxiliary artisans (those who rendered services to the agricultural population, as did shoemakers, smiths, masons, or potters) resembled the peasants in political behavior. But the industrial artisans (weavers, spinners, and dyers) are another problem. Part of the problem is a simple matter of identification, since the most prosperous master weavers are practically indistinguishable from the poorer merchants, while the poorest rarely appear in the available documents. The more serious complication is that weavers and their confreres appeared on both sides of the party line between 1789 and 1793. On the one hand, it is evident that where there were many artisans, there were patriot strongholds. Cholet, Chemillé, Mortagne, and Bressuire are cases in point. Furthermore, a large proportion of the local National Guard companies and of the voluteers from the *bocage* were artisans. This much is evidence of alignment with the patriots. On the other hand, a very large share of the leaders of demonstrations against the patriots in 1791 and 1792, and an exceptional number of local chiefs of the insurrection itself in 1793, were also artisans, for reasons which are now examined.

It is important to note that the textile industry of the *bocage*, after decades of energetic growth, began to falter just about the beginning of the Revolution. . . . The first signs appear in local reports for 1788; at the end of that year the merchants complained that business was falling off. According to the accounts of the most important government bureau, at Cholet, production was down 25 per cent in 1789. . . . In the responses of the communes of Anjou to the 1790 questionnaire of the *Comité de Mendicité* of the *Constituante*, it was precisely those communes and cantons where weaving had flourished that reported the highest proportions of individuals needing assistance. . . . Artisan discontent with this situation broke out in demonstrations against the bourgeois of Chemillé, Trémentines, and other textile centers. In fact, in the district of Cholet—the cradle alike of the textile industry, of resistance to the Revolution before 1793, and of the counterrevolution itself—every locality that reported more than a quarter of its population needing assistance in 1790 was the scene of at least one "insurrection," and a center of exceptional agitation, between then and the counterrevolution. It is therefore not entirely unreasonable to entertain the hypothesis that the industrial artisans were the most discontented class of the *bocage* during the early Revolution, that they expressed their discontent in exceptional political activity, that although at the beginning many of them cast their lot with the Revolution, the fact that the Revolution did

---

[1] Businessmen engaged in foreign trade.—Ed.

much for the merchants and very little for them eventually encouraged a sizable number of them to turn bitterly to the opposition. The virtual absence of industrial artisans in the valley and plain meant that this type of unemployment could not have the same divisive effects in the revolutionary sections of the west as in the counterrevolutionary country of the *bocage*.

This description of party divisions in the *bocage* has one implication that has remained unrecognized too long: the division between *patriote* and *aristocrate* reached into the interior of every locality of the area that joined the counterrevolution. The Revolution made itself felt through the presence of small patriot cities and of a nucleus of patriots in almost every parish of the *bocage*.

As one might expect, it was particularly the cities, centers of trade and industry (such as Montaigu and Cholet), rather than strongholds of the nobility (such as Beaupréau and Châtillon) that breathed patriotic fire. . . .

But it was not just a matter of the scattering of cities, with their spirited patriots and National Guards, through the *bocage*. To understand the ecology of counterrevolution in the Vendean countryside, one must avoid the image of concentrated peasant villages surrounded by fields and substitute for it a picture of a rural community composed of a central settlement, the bourg, usually containing less than half the population, with the rest of the population distributed through tiny villages, hamlets of two or three dwellings, and isolated farms. The bourg's size and importance varied with the amount of commercial and manufacturing activity in the commune, but in every commune the homes and activities of the bourgeois and the artisans were concentrated there. The bourg was the last outpost of the Revolution.

The effect of this arrangement was to divide almost every commune of the *bocage* socially and physically, to make the confrontation and conflict of the two parties an everyday matter, and to heighten the sense of encirclement and desperation of the country patriots. For they, in contrast with their urban comrades, were in direct, constant contact with their political enemies and were frequently the weaker party. The bourgeois of the small cities and bourgs, surrounded by inimical countrymen, beat the patriotic drums all the more loudly, to keep their enemy at a distance and, perhaps, to fortify their own sense of purpose and solidarity. As a result, much of the local history of the early Revolution in the *bocage* is of the clash between country and city and between bourg and hinterland, of the attempt of a small, weak, yet articulate and officially dominant group of urban bourgeois to bring the great changes of 1789 and 1790 to a recalcitrant countryside. Far from being the unanimous voice of an undivided region against an external enemy, the counterrevolution was a cry of vengeance against the enemy within.

Two general observations clarify the tumultuous history of the early Revolution in the *bocage:* the bourgeoisie acquired political power, to the virtual exclusion of all other classes; the dominant fact of the period was a series of conflicts between parties already fairly well defined by early in 1791, a series of which the counterrevolution was the most vicious episode.

The vocabulary of class conflict should not obscure the fact that the immediate issue was rather more political than economic. The rising bourgeois of the *bocage* found themselves in a country where they had little influence over the peasantry, intensely religious, dominated by its curés, where it was usual to say that the priest "governed" his parish. In fact, an extraordinary number of curés of the *bocage* became mayors of their communes at the first elections, in 1790. The bourgeois sought to displace the parish priest of the *bocage* from the political position he had already lost peaceably and imperceptibly, over a long period of time, in the other sections of the west.

The bourgeois won a temporary victory. The Civil Constitution of the Clergy, enacted by the *Constituante* during 1790 and put into motion in the west early in 1791, essentially transformed the parish priest into a civil servant, into an employee of the local political authorities. Indeed, the fact that they had much more to lose, and could count more surely on the support of their parishioners, largely accounts for the greater rate of rejection of the Civil Constitution by the priests of the *bocage* than by those of valley and plain. For the curés of the *bocage*, the oath solicited in January 1791 was not only a question of conscience, but also a question of capitulation to the local bourgeoisie. But the bourgeoisie, backed by the armed force of the nation, succeeded in forcing many of the curés into hiding and the rest into exile and in substituting for them more cooperative priests from elsewhere who had taken the oath.

At the same time, the bourgeois were taking over the political offices offered by the Revolution. It is no news that the clergy were out of office after 1790, since rejection of the oath automatically disqualified the priests. The remarkable feature of the political changes between 1789 and 1792 is the displacement of the peasants by the bourgeoisie. If we compare the deputies to the provincial assemblies for the Estates General of 1789 with the cantonal electors of 1790–1792 in two districts of Anjou, the one (Cholet) the very center of the counterrevolution and the other (Saumur) a solidly revolutionary territory, we find the . . . situation [as shown in the table below]. It would be impetuous to generalize from this one comparison, but it will serve to suggest that the Revolution brought the bourgeois the political positions they desired, and it did so more rapidly in the revolutionary areas than in the counterrevolutionary ones.

Paul Bois, in noticing the decline of the rural electorate, has interpreted these changes as a sign of peasant apathy. The election records, however, indicate that at first the two parties struggled for control of the political machinery and that the later withdrawal of the peasants was more in protest than in disinterest. Two features of the law favored the departure of all *aristocrates* from all electoral as-

| | Cholet | | | | Saumur | | |
Year	Bourgeois	Peasant	Other	Year	Bourgeois	Peasant	Other
1789	57%	38%	5%	1789	62%	28%	10%
1790	64%	22%	14%	1790	88%	9%	3%
1791	80%	4%	16%	1791	89%	–	11%
1792	77%	14%	9%	1792	82%	4%	14%

semblies after 1790: the necessity of being signed up for the National Guard and the requirement of a civic oath. The first was believed to align the citizen with the agents of the Revolution, and the second to signify public acceptance of the Civil Constitution of the Clergy. The year 1791, however, witnessed both the organization of "counterrevolutionary" National Guard companies, who dispensed with the civic oath, as at St. Pierre-de-Chemillé, and electoral assemblies at which the oath was unceremoniously omitted, as at Jallais. . . .

The cantonal elections have received considerable attention because they involved enough people to make some summary statistics feasible and because they named the men who would in turn elect the district and department officials. At the level of district and department, and to a lesser extent at the level of the individual commune, the same eventual dominance by bourgeois patriots took place. The disappearance of the rest of the population from these offices was encouraged by simple unwillingness to do the work of the Revolution, as testifies the frequency with which municipal officers resigned when they were called on to install the constitutional curé.

There is one crucial element to add to this description: the loss of effective control of the population. As the patriots assumed control of local offices, they discovered they did not have the means to do the work of the Revolution. They met passive resistance everywhere, were unable to collect taxes, quell disturbances, protect the constitutional curés. The use of their most powerful weapon, the calling in of the National Guard of one of the region's cities, served in the long run to estrange them further from the popula-

tions they were supposed to govern. . . . Small wonder, then, that the patriots of the little bourgs of the Vendée, with a growing sense of isolation and despair, turned to their urban allies for aid, and by doing so widened the chasm between the parties. They hated and feared each other as only feuding neighbors can.

The account I have given should make clear that the party conflict that eventuated in the struggle of 1793 began long before that "spontaneous" revolt, that it was the irritating presence of the enemy in almost every bourg that gave the conflict much of its bitterness, and that the most important public issue separating the parties was—as it was for a century after the Revolution—the relationship of Church and state. It was at the nearly simultaneous application of the Civil Constitution of the Clergy and sale of Church properties that neutrality became impossible. There is no real distinction between the categories of patriots, supporters of the constitutional clergy, and purchasers of Church properties. In the bocage they were the same group, their core the merchants of the cities and largest bourgs. Outside the bocage few citizens were forced to make a politically significant choice between the old clergy and the new, and a wide range of the population, including peasants, bought Church properties.

It is true that the usual paltry properties of the bocage curé were less tempting than the extensive lands of the religious establishments in the surrounding plains and valleys. Possibly the sentiment of many peasants toward the purchasers was less moral indignation than envy and disappointment, for some peasants did buy during the first few weeks of the sales. In the area that later joined the counterrevolution, nevertheless, the purchase of Church properties was an almost certain sign of alignment with the patriot party.

From that point on, the threat of counterrevolution grew. Most of the conflicts between *patriotes* and *aristocrates* before 1793 were limited in scope and consequences, but there were enough of them, and a sufficient number involving violence or threats of violence to indicate that the matter was serious. In the coastal Vendée alone, for example, in the short period from mid-April to mid-May 1791 there were armed demonstrations against the patriots at Challans, St. Gilles, Palluau, Apremont, St. Jean-des-Monts, Machecoul, and St. Christophe-du-Ligneron. Toward the end of the same year the great processions and pilgrimages that had started as fairly peaceful affirmations of attachment to the old religious order grew much more warlike, becoming occasions for threats and imprecations against the local patriots, and for the display of crude but ominous weapons. The most serious example of the violent encounters between patriots and their enemies that anticipated the counterrevolution was the attack on Châtillon and Bressuire in August 1792, which may have involved as many as six thousand rebels, and left several hundred dead.

In this setting, the violent resistance of the Vendée to conscription in March 1793 is not too difficult to understand. No doubt the boys of the *bocage* did not like the idea of military service, but that fact hardly distinguished them from the youth of the surrounding regions, where the draft proceeded peacefully. It was the first time that the patriots had tried to impose a drastic and unpopular measure on the whole countryside simultaneously; even the deportation of the

clergy had been partial, had operated in irregular stages, and had depended on the cooperation of the priests themselves. This time the fragments of the counterrevolutionary party were able to coalesce.

Furthermore, the law essentially exempted the patriots by excusing public officials and mobilizing the National Guard "in place." In the *bocage* this meant that only the *aristocrates* were eligible. Nothing could have more effectively brought into the open the cleavage between the parties. The people called for the buyers of Church properties and the chiefs of the National Guard to go first. . . . In short, this was the latest and gravest of the series of conflicts between the patriots and aristocrats of the Vendée.

One last observation reinforces the impression of continuity between the party battles of 1791–1792 and the outbreak of the counterrevolution. The first violent events of the counterrevolution were demonstrations by countrymen who disarmed the patriots of their bourgs and then proceeded to do the same to the patriots of the nearest city; events at Cholet, Machecoul, Montaigu, and St. Florent fit this pattern. The first "battles" of the counterrevolution were actually massive but haphazard forays by country people into the patriot bourgs and cities of the Vendée, their prime targets the homes and headquarters of the bourgeois.

Nowhere in this essay will the reader find the old theme of royalism as a "motive" for the Vendée; nor will he find religion in the abstract. This is not to say that the peasants and artisans who rose in March 1793 were indifferent to questions of politics and religion. On the contrary, they cursed the republicans and hailed the *bons prêtres* with ferocious energy. But the unity of the counterrevolutionaries at the beginning of their adventure was rather in opposition to the regional and local patriot minority than in either a common ideology or a theoretical opposition to the Revolution in general. The ideology of the "Catholic and Royal Army" emerged from the stress of battle and from the need of the combatants to explain to themselves and to others what they were doing. It is therefore risky to take the rebels' own later pronouncements for explanations of the counterrevolution.

The strategic questions to ask and answer are not, in fact, doctrinal. They are basically sociological: the special features of the counterrevolutionary areas, the composition of the parties, the conditions that permitted violent opposition to the patriots to develop. Firm answers to questions of this nature require the long, tedious, systematic, even statistical, analysis of masses of documents. But we may anticipate the conclusions of that essential research in at least these respects: the enduring difference in social organization between the revolutionary and counterrevolutionary areas of the west, the Revolution succeeding only where commercial and urban influence, and therefore bourgeois power, had advanced as it had elsewhere in France; the existence of a large number of small, irritating, local patriot parties, limited primarily to the mercantile bourgeoisie; the progressive embitterment of relations between the two contending parties, to the point of violent counterrevolution in 1793.

CRANE BRINTON (1898–1968), long a professor at
Harvard University, was one of America's leading
scholars. He wrote extensively on the problems of
revolution and was one of the first historians to employ
sociological techniques in his research. In this
selection he has investigated an important revolutionary
faction, the Jacobins, in an effort to describe precisely
their social composition, methods of operation, and
political objectives.*

Crane Brinton

Who Were the Jacobins?

Statistics will do more for us than count
the Jacobins by head. Existing documents
are complete enough to permit statistical
treatment of Jacobin wealth, occupation,
birthplace, residence, and age. It is true
that these characteristics are in a sense
external, that they do not necessarily
enter into Jacobinism as a state of mind.
But states of mind cannot be counted;
and a man's wealth, occupation, birthplace, residence and age go far to make
up the man as a political animal—not so
far, perhaps, as the economic interpretation of history would have them go, but
so far that no reasonable historian would
neglect them. From these documents,
then, we ought to be able to place the
normal Jacobin in an economic and social
"class"—decide whether he is upper class,
middle class, or lower class, noble, bourgeois, or proletarian.

But we can perhaps go further, and use
this statistical method to investigate a
sociological question not wholly outside
our search for a definition of Jacobinism.
There is a current theory—or better, a
current opinion—that all violent revolutions are the work of men who are discontented with the society from which
they rebel almost wholly because they
are failures in that society. They are
victims of maladjustment, and this maladjustment, save for a few "misguided
superiors," usually shows itself in economic inferiority. Violent revolutionaries
are poor men, at the very least failures

*Crane Brinton, *The Jacobins: An Essay in the New History* [1930] New York: Russell & Russell, 1961.
Pp. 46–57. Footnotes omitted.

in their life work. Revolutions are essentially risings of the unfit against the fit. . . . At any rate, the maladjustment theory is sufficiently widespread to be worth testing. If then we ask ourselves, were the rank and file of the Jacobin clubs failures or successes in their chosen professions, we can, for the French Revolution at least, give this theory a test.

Our sources of information are adequate enough to permit a statistical answer to this question. Once equipped with information as to the names, residence, age and profession of individual Jacobins in a given club, it is possible to search out these men on the rolls of direct taxes for this locality at the very end of the *ancien régime,* and find out how much they were taxed. By comparing the average Jacobin tax with the average tax paid by non-Jacobins on the same roll, one can place the Jacobins pretty exactly in the common life of their community. Tax rolls of the revolutionary period itself were not always drawn up; and those which have survived are usually hidden away in uncatalogued municipal archives. But millions of francs worth of confiscated property was sold by the government, and lists of buyers of this property are almost everywhere available. We can easily find out how much of this property our Jacobins bought and thus learn how many had surplus funds for such investments.

Such information will not, of course, have even the relative accuracy possible in a study of contemporary demography. Its limitations come out clearly when we attempt to classify the Jacobins by profession. In the first place, the occupation of some is not given at all. Some of these were too young to have a gainful occupation, for the clubs frequently admitted sons of their members from sixteen, and even from twelve years of age. Some were

rentiers, already in the eighteenth century a familiar French figure. Other omissions are to be explained by the carelessness of secretaries in drawing up lists which, after all, are not quite official. At any rate, it is safe to conclude that the category "no occupation given" does not represent a jobless and irresponsible set of poor men. It is not very risky to assume that it includes much the same sort of men as the other groups, and that it can therefore be neglected. But even where occupations are given, all is not clear. The word *négociant,* like the American "business man" implies wealth and social standing greater than that of the *marchand,* best translated by the English "shopkeeper." The difference is between the upper middle class and the lower middle class, and is worth noting; yet the two words are very loosely used, and many a listed *négociant* is merely an aspiring *marchand.* Revolutionary leveling would have none of the old distinctions between *avocat, procureur,* and *notaire,* and the successful barrister and the humble notary are often listed alike as *hommes de loi.* So too an *officier de santé* may be a great surgeon or a mere barber. But the most serious difficulty is with the peasants. Obviously what is most important to know about a peasant is whether he is a landowner, a tenant farmer or a landless agricultural laborer. This it is unfortunately almost impossible to learn from these lists. *Propriétaire, métayer* and *journalier* are perfectly clearly owner, tenant and laborer; but these terms are used much less often than the ambiguous *laboureur, agriculteur,* and *cultivateur,* of which the first usually implies ownership, the last either landlessness or very small property, and the middle nothing at all for our purpose. Thus our classification of the peasantry into owners and nonowners will be very tentative, and best not attempted save for certain localities.

There is still another difficulty. Over the whole course of the Revolution, the personnel of the clubs varied to a considerable degree with the proscription or resignation of moderates and the recruiting of radicals. While it is not true that 1793, the year of the Girondin defeat, marks a complete change in personnel, there certainly was in most clubs a period of renewed energy in the autumn of 1793 which corresponds to a partly renewed membership. We shall then, do well to consider the clubs for which we have statistics in three groups: (1) a group in which all names appearing on the records from the foundation of the clubs to their extinction are included; (2) a group in which only members during the years 1789–1792 are included; (3) a group in which only members during the years 1793–1795 are included. A comparison of the distribution of professions in these groups will afford a rough means of estimating the extent to which, as the Revolution progressed, it recruited its adherents in lower social strata. We must say *rough means,* for in addition to difficulties of identification and calssification mentioned before, it has not been possible to include every club in all three groups. So defective are the records, especially on the membership before 1793, that the investigator must be content with a miscellaneous assortment of clubs. Fortunately, the third group, covering the years 1793–1795 is most numerous, for in these years the Revolution attained its maximum of *social* as opposed to merely *political,* action.

Now, simply from a study of these tables of occupation, certain conclusions may be made as to the social standing of the Jacobins. A few—a very few—of those without occupation were ex-nobles. Study of the proceedings of individual clubs not infrequently discloses the presence even in 1794 of a few noblemen who had succeeded in living down their birth. In Saverne, indeed, the local boss was a noble. When, at the height of the Terror priests and nobles were excluded by law from the clubs, he resigned amid the regrets of his fellow members, and ran the club quite adequately from behind the scenes. But nobles were certainly an exception among the Jacobins, even from the start. For our purposes, they may be dismissed. What really matters is whether, judged by their occupations, the Jacobins deserve to be labeled *bourgeois* or workingmen, whether they were predominantly professional men, merchants, artisans, or laborers. Let us, then, arbitrarily decide that lawyers, priests, teachers, artists and other followers of the liberal professions, business men, shopkeepers and officers are *bourgeois;* that cobblers, masons, carpenters, locksmiths and other artisans, as well as plain soldiers, are members of the working class; and that peasants, since in most clubs they cannot be sorted into landed and landless, should be counted apart. We shall also disregard the category "No profession given," since there is no reason to suppose it comprises men of different social standing from those whose professions are given. The twelve clubs of group I (1789–1795) would then include 62% *bourgeois,* 28% working class, and 10% peasantry; the twelve clubs of group II (1789–1792)—of which six are also in group I—would include 66% *bourgeois,* 26% working class, and 8% peasantry; the forty-two clubs of group III (1793–1795), a period when the social revolution was at its height, would include 57% *bourgeois,* 32% working class, and 11% peasantry. Shopkeepers (grocers, drapers, millers, tailors and such small retail tradesmen) number 12%, 10% and 17% in each group respectively; business men *(négociants),* 7%, 9%, and 8%; professional men, 19%, 24% and 18%. As for the peasants, in ten villages where some sort of line can be drawn between owners of property and non-owners, the proportion is about six to four in favor of the owners, who were no doubt chiefly small proprietors.

This classification must, of course, ignore failure and success. Yet surely a poor lawyer considers himself as much a gentleman, as much a member of the *bourgeoisie* as a rich one. We may safely reckon the professional men and the business men as members of the middle class, many of them, no doubt, as members of the upper middle class. As for the shopkeepers, they are middle class if not in fact at least in aspiration. So, too, are the civil servants and the officers. The land-owning peasantry, as the nineteenth century was to show, are politically members of the middle class. There remain only artisans, landless peasants and common soldiers who can perhaps be said to be politically out of sympathy with *bourgeois* aims. Yet even here, many a man listed as a carpenter or a weaver is really a master craftsman, an employer of workmen, and often more prosperous than many definitely middle-class lawyers.

This weakness our next tables will remedy. If the mason is really a contractor, for instance, and a rich man, he will be taxed accordingly. Yet even here, our statistics cannot aspire to accuracy. First, on the side of the tax rolls, it is well known that the direct taxes of the *ancien régime* were not apportioned strictly according to income. Yet the unfairness of the system has probably been exaggerated by nineteenth century historians who mistook the confusion of the *ancien régime* for injustice; and certainly

even though the very rich were relatively more lightly taxed than the poor, they paid absolutely greater sums. Of the taxes used in constructing these tables, the *vingtième,* a tax on real property, was paid by *roturiers* and *privilégiés* alike, and is generally admitted to have been a fair tax, and hence a good standard of the relative wealth of those who paid it; the *capitation,* originally a graduated poll-tax, was sometimes evaded by the nobility, or at least not paid in due proportion to income; the *taille,* a direct tax on personal income or on real estate, depending on the region, was not paid by nobles, priests or privileged *bourgeois.* Wherever possible, the *vingtième* has been used. Yet even where other taxes are used, the result need not be considered untrustworthy. In the first place, tax rolls of 1790, even though they retain the old names of the taxes, have been fairly assessed under the new régime which began in 1789; secondly, where the new taxes have been used, as for Beauvais and Grenoble, objections to the inequalities of the older ones no longer hold. Again, even for the *taille,* where property owned by nobles was commercially exploited, it was taxed just as ordinary property, landed or not. Usually the tenant paid the tax, even though it was listed in the noble's name on the roll. Yet nobles did actually sometimes pay the *taille* themselves. See for instance at Rodez, where a record of payments appears on the roll. Finally, the sort of omission from rolls of *capitation* and *taille* in 1789 and earlier years are precisely the sort that will leave the prosperity of the Jacobins underestimated rather than overestimated. For from these rolls the *privilégiés* are omitted and the average payment made by the Jacobins will be the less by our inability to trace the payments of privileged Jacobins. On the side of the lists of members, too, there are difficulties. Many members are not sufficiently identified to be traced further, since neither Christian name nor professions are always given. Many members had moved into the town since the tax roll was drawn up, and cannot therefore be found on it. Many were too young when the roll was made, or not heads of families or owners of property in their own right. Finally, errors of identification are easily possible, though these are in some way compensating—that is to say, as many Jacobins would normally be mistaken for non-Jacobins as non-Jacobins for Jacobins.

The result of a study of these tax rolls is to confirm what was already indicated by Jacobin occupations. In many towns, a list of the poor and incapacitated follows the tax roll; in others, the poor are listed with their fellow citizens, but their names are followed by the entry "no tax" *(néant)*. The names of Jacobins are almost never found among these poor. . . .

The total assessment of all Jacobins traceable on the tax roll can be divided by the total number of members on the club books, *those who were assessed the tax as well as those who were not.* Then the sum total assessed on the town can be divided by the total number of adult males in the town, *those who were assessed the tax as well as those who were not.* Thus the average for the Jacobin club as a whole may be compared with the average for the town as a whole. By this method, a definite cross-section of both the smaller and larger groups is obtained, and we avoid the reproach that no account has been taken of the large number of Jacobins (about one-half) not traceable on the rolls. This method gives, for eight clubs considered over the whole period 1789 to 1795, an average payment of 32.12 livres for the Jacobins, and an average payment of 17.02 livres for all the male citizens of the town; for twenty-six clubs

considered over the period 1793 to 1795, an average payment of 19.94 livres for the Jacobins, and 14.45 livres for all the male citizens. . . .

One tax deserves special consideration. This is the *vingtième d'industrie,* a small but very fair tax assessed on all save civil servants who pursued a gainful occupation. Naturally, this excluded the nobles and the priests. The tax was so small that the total assessed does not vary greatly, ranging usually from one livre to twelve or so. But the apprentice or journeyman always pays a minimum, the master more, the merchant and business man still more. Unfortunately rolls giving individual names are rare, for the various guilds usually subscribed for a definite sum, and then apportioned this sum themselves among their members. These guild rolls are very hard to find. But Table X[1] covers all occupations, or certain trades, in eight typical provincial towns, and does give a certain basis for conclusions. It shows that the average Jacobin paid 4.47 livres as his *vingtième d'industrie,* the average non-Jacobin, 2.49 livres. Clearly, then, among the shopkeepers and artisans, the more prosperous ones were the ones who were active revolutionists. The Jacobin carpenter was not a poor carpenter, but a good one; the steady master workmen outnumber the wild young apprentices in the clubs.

Too much is not to be concluded from our next table, based on purchases of the *biens nationaux.* The Jacobins who bought property—mostly land—confiscated from nobleman and priests had perhaps enriched themselves in ways familiar to politicians, revolutionary or not. Still, they appear to have been a bit too numerous to have been grafters

[1] Crane Brinton has drawn up statistical tables from relevant archival sources. These are included in the work from which this selection is reprinted. —Ed.

to a man; and we can at least be sure that men who invested money in land are not likely to have been communists at heart. Moreover, these tables have a certain interest for students of the disposition of the *biens nationaux,* for they help to show how far the buyers actively identified themselves with the Revolution. In thirteen towns, 763 Jacobins—over one-fifth of the total club membership—bought on an average property to the amount of 14,181 livres. Non-Jacobins to the number of 817 bought an average property of 5,650 livres. In four towns—Colmar, Noviant-aux-Prés, Perpignan, Toul—the number of non-Jacobin buyers exceeded that of Jacobin buyers. Only in one, however—Vesoul—did the average sum expended by the non-Jacobins exceed that expended by the Jacobins. And in Vesoul the non-Jacobin average is high because of the very great purchases of a single buyer, whose name does not appear on the list of members in 1795, but who almost certainly was a member in the early years of the club's existence. Table XII, finally, shows that 517 members out of a total membership of 2,160 in six towns bought property, the amount of which could not be estimated conveniently from existing records. Thus, for the nineteen clubs included in Tables XI and XII, 22% of the membership were buyers of *biens nationaux.* This again confirms the economic prosperity of the Jacobins.

Finally, there are two other bits of information available which serve to indicate the social responsibilities of the group of Jacobins. The first is the age of their members. For ten clubs considered the average age varies very little, from 38.3 years to 45.4 years. The average for the group of ten was 41.8 years. There were some boys in each club, but almost always the sons of prominent members. As can be seen from the average age, the young were quite balanced by the old. In no sense can these clubs be considered a collection of foolhardy young men. The second bit of information concerns the birthplace and actual residence of the members. For twenty-three clubs, the lists of memberships, drawn up mostly at the very end of 1794 show that 2,359 were born in the town in which they were living, and that 1,456 were born elsewhere; for fifteen of these clubs the lists show that 2,571 were resident in the same place before and after 1789, and that 378 had moved into their actual place of residence after 1789—that is, since the Revolution. Too much again must not be concluded from this fragmentary evidence. We do not know for just what proportion of the population of eighteenth century France birthplace and residence coincided, but it would seem that the 3,815 members of the Jacobin clubs above studied numbered rather more immigrants (38%) than the towns in which they were established. No doubt most of these immigrants came from nearby places, and were often country people who had moved to town; but the point is that they had moved. Sociologists may still dispute as to whether emigration indicates initiative or irresponsibility, but to judge from evidence of tax-lists, these emigrants had been successful. As to the second item, the fact that only 378 out of 2,949, or 13%, had moved into the towns since 1789 would show that the Revolution was not fathered largely by itinerant and more or less professional trouble-makers, but by men who knew the surroundings in which they worked.

MICHAEL J. SYDENHAM has written a careful
study of the Girondin faction. After a detailed
analysis of individuals associated with this group, he
raises serious questions about the traditional
interpretation, which viewed the Girondins as an
organized political party. He has also written *The
French Revolution* (1965), a history for the general
reader incorporating much recent research.*

Michael J. Sydenham

Was There a Girondin Party?

The conception of the Girondins as a large and integrated party, apparently derived in part from Jacobin propaganda, has been fostered also by the deceptive ease with which a list of "party supporters" can be compiled from the names of those whom the Montagnards proscribed.

This method was adopted without reserve by Morse Stephens, for whom "the only way to get a true idea of the leaders and the rank and file of the Girondin party" was "from an examination of the proscription lists drawn up against them." Aulard and Claude Perroud both acted on the same principle. Mathiez, on the other hand, did not accept these lists as adequate criteria of party allegiance, and pointed out that only a careful ex-amination of the deputies' actions and votes could provide any valid basis for classification. He did not, however, attempt to draw up a list in this way himself, but tended rather to use the name "Girondin" loosely, and sometimes applied it even to members of the Convention who are not generally so called.

The use of the proscription lists to establish *previous* party membership is in fact essentially unsound. It either presents a picture of a party at the very time when it had for all practical purposes ceased to exist—if, indeed, it had ever existed at all—or it simply confuses opposition to the Mountain at one time with opposition to it at another. Nevertheless, the lists at least indicate the extent of the traditional party, and so their

*Michael J. Sydenham, *The Girondins* (London: Athlone Press, 1964), pp. 39, 207–212. Footnotes omitted.

growth and subsequent consolidation may usefully be reviewed.

The attempt that has been made in [the body of the book] to draw closer to Brissot and his friends has shown that current generalizations on the subject need some revision, and this revision in its turn is not without importance in the interpretation of the general course of the Revolution.

The closer approach, originally suggested by the doubts and differences which are apparent in the historians' views about the unity and policy of the supposed Girondin party, has revealed that its very existence is a remarkable historical legend, originating in contemporary propaganda and subsequently accepted by historians as a matter of convenience. Under examination, the party disintegrates. Proscription by the Montagnards, which has long been accepted as a criterion of membership of the party, has proved to be a fortuitous process from which no valid deductions can be drawn. In practice, there was neither a recognized party leader nor an accepted policy. The supposed Girondin deputies consistently asserted their independence, speaking and acting as individuals even at the most critical moments of the conflict with Robespierre. As for the alleged party headquarters, they have appeared as irrelevant to the main question. When the *Club de la Réunion* was influential it was as much Robespierrist as Brissotin in composition, and a subsequent attempt by Brissot's friends to capture and maintain or develop it was a complete failure. The *Comité Valazé*, the nearest approach to an attempt at party organization, represents nothing more than an ineffectual effort by a comparatively unimportant deputy to rally even more obscure men against the threat of domination by the Montagnard minority. In short, the only people in the Convention to bear any resemblance to a coherent party were the Montagnards, who were opposed by most of the amorphous majority of the assembly.

Brissot and his friends should be regarded as a small and loose-knit group or coalition of individualists who rapidly became representative of the resistance of the majority to Robespierre, their personal independence remaining unqualified. Evidence even of collaboration between them during the time of the Convention is extremely slight, for the meetings at Madame Roland's salon lacked any precision of purpose and ended when her husband resigned his office in January 1793. They appear in the Legislative Assembly as a fairly coherent group, but one of only some seven or eight prominent radicals, a coterie which increased little in size in the Convention. Even in May 1793, when Montagnard pressure was greatest, the "faction" was no more than a frail alliance of some fifteen deputies, men whose outlook was so identical with that of the majority of their colleagues that they can be distinguished only as personalities, individuals whose reputation, powers of oratory or personal courage marked them out above others as enemies of the Mountain.

A group of this sort can scarcely be said to have had any specific policy. The men concerned, however, may be regarded as representing in some respects a great many of the revolutionaries. Most of them were clearly *arrivistes,* drawn together even before 1789 by their profound dissatisfaction with the society in which they lived. In their letters, in Brissot's *Patriote français* and at Madame Roland's first receptions, they had expressed their discontent with the existing order and anticipated the opening of a new era. When their opportunity occurred in 1791–2 they showed themselves avid and irresponsible in their pursuit of place and power, even to the extent of encouraging incipient insurrection in order to gain political advantage. Then, when leadership had been won, they proved irresolute in everything but the endeavour to retain it, vacillating at all critical times and showing determination only in their efforts to crush Robespierre, the man who impugned their integrity and challenged their authority.

Yet even in these, their most unpleasing characteristics—which were of course by no means peculiar to them—Brissot and his friends were not altogether unpardonable. They seem to have sought power more for its social advantages than from any desire to dominate. Some of them indeed acted as demagogues, stimulating forces which they were quite unable to control, but they were not themselves serious enemies of society. Rather were they men of considerable culture and professional ability, who had hitherto been excluded from their appropriate place in the political and social life of the nation. Before the Revolution, their political energies were confined to impracticable plans for philanthropy in France and to participation in the remote cause of negro emancipation overseas, while their social aspirations could only be expressed by the assumption of such trivial territorial titles as Brissot *de Warville,* Pétion *de Villeneuve,* and Roland *de la Platière.* By 1792, however, they had gained the social status appropriate to their new political position. They were, for a time, cultivated by the liberal nobility. Pétion became Mayor of Paris. Ministers of State sat at Madame Roland's table. Their salons seemed to stand at the centre of French affairs. It

is understandable if for them the Revolution was, in a sense, consummated.

Although Robespierre's quarrel with Brissot began when he refused to acknowledge the expediency of an attack upon Austria, the root of his hostility towards the Brissotins lay in his recognition of their readiness to accept the Revolution as completed, to consort with men of rank and reputation, and so to sever themselves from the still unsatisfied lower ranks of the people. The quarrel, in its turn, revealed a second respect in which Brissot and his friends represented a common contemporary attitude: as ample evidence, particularly that of the debate at the Jacobin Society on 26 March 1792, indicates, their philosophy was a somewhat cynical deism. In this they were sharply distinguished from Robespierre, who regarded the Revolution as one through which Providence was working to eradicate every evil from society and to bring about the complete regeneration of mankind.

This distinction had far-reaching consequences in the development both of the Revolution and of France. At first their lack of a more positive faith merely encouraged Brissot and his friends to procrastinate in emergencies and, instead of seeking positive solutions, to resort to the repression of social and political unrest. Later, however, the very limitations of their outlook acquired a positive value. Although they themselves lived precariously from day to day, having no immediate object save the elimination of Robespierre, their opposition to him made them, almost inadvertently, the champions of two fundamental principles. They came to represent both the Rule of Law and the right of the individual to resist oppression by the State.

After the insurrection of 10 August

1792, revolutionary authority, exercised in the name of the sovereign people, was retained by .the Commune of Paris in defiance of the rump of the Legislative Assembly. The friends of Brissot, particularly the deputies of the Gironde, then attempted to restore some sort of constitutional authority by calling for a national Convention and by attempting to dissolve the Commune. The Convention, however, was in its turn confronted by the refusal of the Paris radicals to acknowledge its authority. This may have been in some measure a consequence of the Brissotins' exploitation of their influence in the new assembly in their effort to discredit and destroy Robespierre, but it was nevertheless a clear instance of the defiance of a legally constituted authority by a dissident minority of the people, even if it was adopted after provocation and in support of what were believed to be progressive principles. Robespierre himself did not finally sanction the forcible seizure of power by the radical minority of Paris until he considered that the nation stood in such danger that the action was justified, yet he had long lent his prestige to a parallel course—the systematic perversion of parliamentary procedure by the Montagnard minority. Both the Montagnards, in their defiance of majority decisions, and the Brissotin leaders of the majority, in their attacks upon Robespierre and their appeals to the provincial electorate, were putting into practice a conception of democracy not compatible with the Rule of Law, but as the Brissotins' fight to maintain their position against the threats of the Jacobins, the Commune and the crowd became increasingly futile, they became increasingly conscious of the virtues of legality and the iniquity of the appeal to violence.

Their failure to deal effectively with the radicals of Paris must yet stand as the most serious failure of these men. The opening of the Convention appears in French history as a moment of great opportunity, which constructive statesmen might have employed to reconcile the people of Paris to the rule of an assembly lawfully elected by a more conservative countryside. Far from attempting this difficult task, those who led the majority first antagonized Paris by persecuting its delegates, and then fostered the latent hostility between the capital and the provinces by futile attempts to enlist provincial aid in their own interest. The ensuing crisis was checked by the Terror and by the Montagnards' alliance with the radicals of Paris, but this alliance was but a temporary incident, and Robespierre himself was to be overthrown in his turn in part because he too tried to restrain the radicals. The conflict between the national assembly and the *sans-culottes* was not again resolved until Napoleon did what Brissot and the deputies of the Gironde had lacked the power or the decision to do, and dispersed the mob with his "whiff of grapeshot." But even Napoleon could not wholly heal the wounds which these events inflicted upon France, and subsequent struggles kept them open and angry throughout the nineteenth century.

On the other hand, those who led the Convention before Robespierre's advent to power deserve praise for their refusal to recognize the validity of the doctrines which were implicit in the *coup d'état* which drove them from the assembly. In the end they took their stand upon principle, though they only became conscious of it when their own lives were at stake and they were faced with the consequences of the contrary principle. For Robespierre's eventual decision to sanction revolutionary action by the *sans-culottes* was in large measure a consequence of his personal philosophy. By May 1793 he had come to the conclusion that the Revolution was being endangered by a self-interested clique. From his philosophy it followed that this same clique was frustrating the purposes of Providence, of which, by approving the purge of the Convention, he made himself the arbiter. Thereafter, by refusing to recognize the legality of Robespierre's victory, the deputies who were driven from their seats were really resisting the doctrine that an *élite* has the right to rule by virtue of its understanding of the way in which the State may bring men spiritual salvation as well as material welfare. Eventually those deputies who died in 1793–4 died in defence of a vital principle: by challenging the authority of the court which condemned them in the sinister name of the security of the State, they really proclaimed their faith in a Republic which would approve and defend individual freedom of conscience.

They did not die in vain. After only a year, the ruthless rule of Robespierre's *élite* proved as unnecessary as it was intolerable, and when the survivors of those who were proscribed in 1793 returned to the Convention after Thermidor, France had resumed the line of political development most natural to her people. Some later historians have indeed paid lip-service to Michelet's interpretation of the Revolution as Justice incarnate, and said as he did of those who died that "the divine fire of the Revolution was not in them": but since the days of the Jacobins no such *élite* has obtained power in France, and the nation's most serious weakness has remained that so apparent among the leaders of the Convention—an excess of individualism.

ROBERT R. PALMER (b. 1909), currently at Yale
University, has written numerous works on the French
Revolution, including an excellent study of the
Committee of Public Safety. He has also studied the
development of revolutionary movements outside of
France and the relationship between French and foreign
revolutionaries. In this selection he deals with the
Committee of Public Safety, its reaction to the crisis
of 1793–1794, and its attitude toward foreign radicals.*

Robert R. Palmer

The Terror: A Response to Crisis

The issue, for France and the world in
1793, was not whether one band of Jacobins should chase out another, but
whether Revolution or Counter-Revolution should prevail.

It was true that France at the moment
suffered from anarchy, and that what it
needed was government. "Anarchy" is
hardly too strong a word. Ministers and
ministries remained in existence, but
decisions lay with committees of the Convention, which consisted of 750 men from
the middle classes assembled under
chaotic conditions, and enjoying neither
confidence in each other, nor the prestige
of an acknowledged authority, nor habits
of obedience on the part of the population. Organs of local government, as set

up in 1790 and 1791, had not had time to
consolidate. Tax reforms of the early
years of the Revolution had also been
caught unfinished by the war and the
upheaval of 1792. Taxes, like much else,
existed mainly in principle. There were
no regular revenues, so that the Convention depended on paper money. Army
reforms, begun early in the Revolution,
had also been far from complete; the
country went to war with its armies commanded largely by officers of the Old
Régime; and as the revolutionary spirit
mounted into 1793, the officers increasingly lost respect for the civilians in
Paris who claimed to govern. Dumouriez
was only the most spectacular case.

Impotence in what would normally

*"The Struggle," Vol. II from *The Age of the Democratic Revolution: A Political History of Europe and America, 1760–1800,* by R. R. Palmer (Copyright © 1964 by Princeton University Press), pp. 102–113. Reprinted by permission of Princeton University Press and Oxford University Press. Footnotes omitted.

be considered the government was matched by an intense political liveliness among the "governed." It was a question whether the country could be governed at all, except by dictatorship, whether a revolutionary dictatorship such as soon developed, or the dictatorship of a restored king, such as the moderate Mounier, writing in exile, had recommended in 1792. The French people in 1793 were too highly politicized, too spontaneously active, too disillusioned with persons in public office (not without reason), to accept orders from any political heights. When they said the people were sovereign, they meant it literally, and they meant themselves. Middle class citizens, associated in the Paris Jacobin club and in similar clubs in the provinces, and acting on their own initiative, tried somehow to keep going, coordinate, and dominate the shattered apparatus of state, from the National Convention down to the village communes. Citizens of more modest station . . . met in lesser clubs, like the Paris Cordeliers, or in the face-to-face groups of immediate neighbors, as in the section assemblies of Paris and other large cities. They too, at the local level, helped to carry on the business of government.

The people were not only sovereign but *debout,* "on their feet," to use the expression of the time. Popular leaders called for a *levée en masse,* or general "rising." The term *levée en masse* has become frozen to signify the universal military service of the Revolution, a conscription conducted by government and designed to expel foreign invaders. It is true that the military *levée en masse* would not have been very effective if it had not been converted into an organized raising and equipping of troops by a government. But in its origin the term meant much more. A "mass rising," in 1793, could be a general rising of the people for any purpose, with or without the assistance of official persons who did not command much public confidence. It could be a swarming of citizen soldiers to defy the regular armies of Prussia and Austria. It could be a rising of the sections of Paris against the Convention or some of its members. It could be an armed insurrection or an unarmed demonstration in the streets. It could be the wandering of a band of sans-culottes from one part of France to another, self-organized as an *armée révolutionnaire,* in pursuit of aristocrats or in search of food. There was something inherently anarchic in the whole idea.

Out of this anarchy there arose, however, by gradual stages, the *gouvernement révolutionnaire,* confirmed by the Convention in a famous decree of October 10, 1793, declaring "the government of France revolutionary until the peace." It began with an at first little noticed provision, when on April 6, the day after Dumouriez' final defection, the Convention authorized a special Committee of Public Safety, which in six months became the keystone of the *gouvernement révolutionnaire.* It was this government, which lasted until the death of Robespierre, and which Napoleon once called the only serious government in France in the decade after 1789, that turned the tide of foreign invasion, carried on the Terror, protected the country from both anarchy and counter-revolution, and initiated the military offensive which was to revolutionize Holland and Italy and shake the established order of Europe.

For the purposes of this book, it is of especial interest to trace the relations of this Revolutionary Government with popular revolutionism and with international revolutionism. Pressures generated by both these movements helped to bring the Revolutionary Government into being. Once established, it sought to subordinate both movements to itself.

Between the two, . . . there was often a certain affinity. It was not that the popular spokesmen in Paris cared much about revolution in foreign countries. Still less, in general, did the foreign revolutionaries understand or know much about the demands of the most advanced revolutionaries in Paris. Usually, however, both had much to complain of at the hands of the French revolutionary authorities. In March and April 1793 the Brissot-Dumouriez group, despite Dumouriez' disaffection, was still preponderant in the committees of the Convention. The international revolutionaries blamed them for the defeats and failures in Belgium and Holland. (Much less concern was expressed for Poland, although Kosciuszko was in Paris at this very time to solicit aid.) The popular revolutionaries were annoyed by the defeats also, which were bringing the enemy within the gates, and in addition they suffered the effects of food shortage and inflation. An extreme crisis of confidence in the political realm coincided with an extreme economic crisis. In the inflamed psychology of the moment, both crises were blamed on the same people. Suspicion was rampant. The guilty must be investigated and pursued. In March the Convention created a new special court for this purpose, the Revolutionary Tribunal, in which the civil liberties and legal reforms introduced by the Revolution could be suspended.

An enlightening history of the Revolution in France could be written in terms of the paper money alone, the *assignats.* For the political and social consolidation of the Revolution the program proved highly successful. In the absence of gold coinage (which was hoarded, or taken out of the country by émigrés, or used in connection with foreign payments), the paper money enabled the successive Revolutionary governing groups to finance their operations. It also provided the mechanism for the transfer of former church, crown, and émigré real estate to new owners, blending the upper levels of the peasantry, the bourgeoisie, and many ex-nobles into a numerous property-owning class of modern type, which had a material interest in the preservation of the Revolutionary innovations.

But the costs of war led to a rapid printing of assignats, which steadily lost value, especially since the future of the régime that printed them was highly uncertain. The decline was precipitous in the first half of 1793, when the assignats fell to only a fourth the value of gold. There were also positive scarcities. As causes of scarcity, to the normal effects of war and mobilization, and unwillingness of farmers to part with their produce for paper money, was added a general breakdown in commercial distribution in the confusion of revolutionary conditions. Prices soared. Bakeshops and grocers' shops were often found empty by women who had waited for hours to obtain a day's supply.

There were therefore demands for price controls, and for measures against hoarding and profiteering. By attributing these demands specifically to the working class, and resistance to them to the bourgeoisie, various historians have seen this period of the Revolution as characterized chiefly by a class conflict, of a kind that relates it to the socialisms of the twentieth century. It is true that the Brissot group, setting the tone in the Convention, objected to economic controls. They had fallen into an attitude of negativism and helplessness toward everything that had happened since the preceding August.

The idea of price control was not in itself very radical. The monarchy had practiced it before 1789, and even the weakly organized American states, during the American Revolution, had made similar attempts in the face of inflation. So bourgeois a figure as Alexander Hamilton, in 1778, had been as incensed at profiteering as a Paris sans-culotte of 1793. But what for Hamilton and middle-class people was a matter for moral indignation, was for the working people of Paris a matter of life and death. The sections of Paris seethed with protest. There developed a great *poussée populaire,* as Albert Soboul calls it, a rising tide of the popular democracy . . . against the "corrupt" element in the Convention.

Early in April the Section Halle au Blé circulated among the other sections of the city a proposed petition to the Convention. Halle au Blé was not a poor section; indeed, it had the fewest "indigent" of any of the forty-eight. It demanded action against hoarders, speculators, and monopolists. Still more vehemently, it accused the Convention of endless talk and insidious treachery. The proof lay in Dumouriez' whole record in Belgium. If the Convention had not protected Dumouriez and his accomplices, so ran the indictment, "the Belgians and Liégeois would not today accuse France of having aided them only to turn them over in chains to their tyrants. It is with this that all Europe reproaches you, and posterity will do the same." The petition demanded the arrest of certain Brissotins, i.e., a purge of the Convention.

Robespierre defended the petition at the Jacobin Club and in the Convention. He paid little attention to the economic demands. It was treason that he scented, and for proof he pointed to the betrayal of the international revolution. He now sympathized with the *patriotes bataves*

and the *braves Liégeois.* Why had not Dumouriez pursued and destroyed the Prussians after Valmy? Why had the Belgian Democrats been blocked by him at every turn? Why had he not sooner and more vigorously carried the war into Holland? . . . Had he seriously invaded Holland, France would now have the use of Dutch wealth and shipping, so that England would be ruined, and "the revolution of Europe would be assured." (This had been precisely the argument of the Dutch émigrés in December and January, which Robespierre himself had then opposed.) But no, the Brissot-Dumouriez group had never favored international revolution. They had disapproved of the annexation of Savoy and Belgium, betrayed the Dutch, tried "to halt the progress of our revolution in neighboring countries." In addition, they were suspiciously close to their friend Philippe Egalité, the *ci-devant* Duke of Orleans. Why had this person's son (the future King Louis-Philippe, who later boasted of having fought at Valmy) been commissioned as a lieutenant-general at the age of nineteen? What kind of officers were in this republican army anyway? Brissot, according to Robespierre, now really wanted to make peace with the foreign powers, with a restoration of monarchy in the Orleans line.

Anyone living in the democratized twentieth century knows that there can be no public talk of peace in time of war. There could be no talk of peace for Robespierre, especially if it meant a relapse into monarchy. He demanded the death penalty for anyone suggesting compromise with the enemy. This proposal, amended in the Convention by Danton, who favored private overtures to the enemy, turned into a well-known decree, by which France was supposed (at least by historians) to "renounce" the two

Propaganda Decrees of 1792, which, as already explained, were not really "propaganda" decrees at all. The Convention now declared that it would not interfere with the government of other powers, but that these powers must not interfere in the affairs of France and its constitution; and that anyone favoring compromise with the enemy should be put to death, *unless* the enemy, in advance, recognized "the sovereignty, independence, indivisibility and unity of the Republic, founded on liberty and equality." This left matters not actually much changed, since the powers had not yet made clear any such bland intentions.

Meanwhile the Convention, an incredible body, at war with all Europe, with its commanding general in Belgium proved disloyal, with peasants in armed rebellion in the West, with the currency out of control, the economy collapsing, and the popular agitation in the Paris sections boiling over, found moments to engage in its theoretically principal business, to "constitute" a regular government through a new written constitution and declaration of rights. The committee on the constitution was dominated by Condorcet and other Brissotins or Girondists. There was much on which they did not disagree with the Mountain, notably universal suffrage, universal schooling, public relief to the needy, and other attributes of a democratic state. Robespierre, however, was convinced that the Girondists were unfit to govern. He made an issue over their proposed Declaration of Rights. On April 24 he submitted and explained to the Convention a draft Declaration of his own. Though never adopted, it is a key document to the understanding of his thinking and his tactics.

For one thing, where the Girondist draft would limit resistance to government to "legal" channels, Robespierre was more indulgent to the right of insurrection. This meant, in the political realities of the moment, that Robespierre supported the dynamism of the sansculottes in the Paris sections against the convention. Not yet in power himself, he was more sympathetic to "direct democracy" than he would be later.

He also called for the addition of two groups of new articles to the Declaration of Rights. The first group, composed of five articles, referred to the right of property, and touched on the ideology of popular revolution. The second group, in four articles, referred to international fraternization, and touched on the matter of international revolutionism.

Robespierre, like the popular democrats, favored a degree of economic equality which he never specified, but which fell short of the equality of incomes that Babeuf demanded three years later. "Equality of wealth is a chimera," he said, "necessary neither to private happiness nor to the public welfare." But "the world hardly needed a revolution to learn that extreme disproportion of wealth is the source of many evils." He proposed, therefore, to lay it down as a principle that property right was a creation of law, not of nature apart from law, and that, like liberty, it was inseparable from considerations of ethics, and found its limits where it touched on the rights of others. He also proposed a progressive income tax. Brissot objected, and praise for Robespierre on this score has come more from posterity than from his contemporaries. Since there was no discussion of actual rates, it is hard to estimate the social significance of Robespierre's idea of a progressive tax. He himself soon changed his mind, coming to believe that in a democratic society it was better for men of small means to carry a proportionate share of the costs, lest the well-to-do, by supplying the money, make themselves too indispensable to the state. That he was something of a social as well as a political democrat there can be no doubt.

He appealed also to the force of world revolution, which he now blamed the Girondists for ignoring. He scorned the argument that to stir up the peoples might aggravate the trouble with kings. "I confess that this inconvenience does not frighten me." The kings were already combined against France and against liberty everywhere. "All men of all countries are brothers." They should lend mutual aid as if they were citizens of a single state. The oppressor of one nation is the enemy of all. "Kings, aristocrats and tyrants, of every description, are slaves in revolt against the sovereign of the earth, which is the human race, and against the legislator of the world, which is nature." "Verbiage pretending to profundity," said Brissot, who had done as much as anyone to introduce such language into French politics since 1789.

In time of war and defeat, against the Brissotins in the Convention, and against the cosmopolitan forces of Counter-Revolution, Robespierre was willing to ally himself with two spirits that have never since been quite conjured away: those of mass upheaval and world revolution.

The Paris sections exploded in May. The Convention enacted controls on the retail price of bread. Agitation continued, sponsored by Jacobins of the Mountain. On May 31 a rising of *sectionnaires* captured the city government, and on June 2 eighty thousand armed sans-culottes besieged the Convention, demanding the arrest of twenty-two of its members. Defenseless and divided, the Convention yielded. Brissot and his friends were

arrested (or fled, like Condorcet), to be disposed of by the Revolutionary Tribunal. The same kind of popular rising which by overthrowing the monarchy in 1792 had brought the Convention into being now threatened the Convention itself in 1793. It remained to be seen whether the Jacobins of the Mountain could avoid the fate of those of the "Gironde."

A constitution was thrown together in a few days. Full of elaborately democratic provisions, it came to be known as the Constitution of the Year I—that is, the first year of the Republic. The primary assemblies, throughout the country, ratified it with a vote reported as 1,801,918 to 11,610, out of some seven million adult men over 21. (Neither the French constitution of 1789–1791, nor the American federal constitution of 1787, had even been offered for direct popular ratification at all.) The Convention, given the facts of war and revolution, made no move to put the constitution into effect, seeming rather to envisage its own indefinite continuation. It appears that the mass of sans-culottes and *sectionnaires* accepted this decision, seeing in the Convention, now purged of its Girondist leadership, a necessary center and symbol of government in time of emergency. Immediately, however, voices were heard demanding the introduction of constitutional government. They came from journalists and militants, like Hébert, who were not members of the Convention and who really meant, not constitutionality, but the dissolution of the Convention and overthrow of Robespierre. Robespierre coined the term "ultrarevolutionary" to describe these men. In the logic of revolution, as he understood it, ultra-revolution came to be an insidious form of counterrevolution. Was he merely setting himself up as a norm? Was he simply identifying his own purposes with "the Revolution"? Was he only resisting the fate he had meted out to Brissot? It does not seem so. To purge the Convention was one thing; to dissolve it, another. The logic of revolution is not altogether weird or subjective, and demands for dissolution of the Convention in 1793, as voiced on the Left, would produce exactly what the most unregenerate conservatives throughout Europe most desired. It can be considered as certain that France could not be governed in 1793 by liberal or democratic constitutional means. To disband the Convention could only perpetuate anarchy. In that case a monarchist restoration, even if it masked a clerico-aristocratic dictatorship, would be welcomed.

That Robespierre could now detect "ultras" was a sign that he was turning from insurrectionism to *gouvernement révolutionnaire*, and that he himself had a hand in this incipient government. In July the Convention elected him to its Committee of Public Safety. But matters had never been worse for the Convention than in this summer of 1793. Marat was assassinated in his bath. He was the second member of the Convention to be assassinated since January. The great provincial cities, Lyon, Marseille, Bordeaux, where the expulsion of the Girondists angered the urban bourgeoisie, denounced the anarchy in Paris and defied the authority of the Convention. This "federalist" rebellion was of course a sign of anarchy in itself, and was abetted by the secret maneuvers of true counter-revolutionaries and foreign agents. At the end of August the royalists at Toulon threw the city open to the British and surrendered the fleet. Edmund Burke demanded that the Allies, now that they had a foothold in southern France, recognize a royal government and make

clear their common cause with the émigrés—the true people of France, as he called them (estimating their number at 70,000), the revolutionaries being "robbers" who had driven them from the house. The powers did not take his advice. They wished a free hand in what seemed an imminent victory.

In Paris the sans-culottes again invaded the Convention on September 4. The Revolutionary Government was the outcome. It rested on a compromise between the popular democrats of the sections and middle-class Jacobins of the Mountain in the Convention. The Convention saved itself from further purging or dissolution, but only by accepting the demands of the populace, in which hysteria, suspicion, fear, revenge, resolution, and patriotic defiance were mixed together. The Convention authorized a *levée en masse* to enlarge the army. It consented reluctantly to a semi-military *armée révolutionnaire* to patrol the country. It enacted the General Maximum, a system of nation-wide price controls on a wide range of consumers' goods. It promised to rid the army of unreliable officers. It passed a draconian Law of Suspects, and enlarged the Revolutionary Tribunal. The Terror began in earnest, as the Brissotins, Marie Antoinette, and various unsuccessful generals went to the guillotine. A Republican Calendar was adopted, marking the end of the Christian Era, and the beginning of the movement known as Dechristianization. In this, as in some other measures, it was only a small minority that called for such extreme action. But it was dangerous and impossible at such a time, opening the way to suspicion and denunciation, for anyone to question the demands of the most intransigently patriotic.

On the other hand, the government began to govern. The Committee of Public

Safety received larger powers. Its membership settled at twelve, who remained the same twelve individuals from September 1793 to July 1794. They included Robespierre, Saint-Just, Couthon, Barère, and Lazare Carnot. The Committee of General Security obtained wide powers of political police, and gradually subordinated the local and largely spontaneous "surveillance committees" to itself. The government was declared "revolutionary until the peace." That is, the question of constitutionality was suspended for the duration. Members of the Convention, despatched to the provinces, to insurgent areas, and to the armies, reported directly to the Committee of Public Safety. This network of *représentants en mission* coordinated and enforced national policy, and worked to assure some measure of uniform loyalty to the Revolution. In December the ruling Committee received powers of appointment and removal of local office-holders throughout the country. A Subsistence Commission, building on the price-controls, and working under the ruling Committee, developed an elaborate system of requisitions, priorities, and currency regulations. The value of the assignat was held steady. The armies were supplied, while Carnot supervised their mobilization and training. By the end of 1793 the Vendéan rebellion was neutralized, the federalist rebellions suppressed, and the British ejected from Toulon. By the spring of 1794 an army of almost a million men faced the foreign enemy. It was the first mass or "democratic" army, or at least the first above the level of casual militia,

possessed of a modern kind of national consciousness, with its morale heightened by political attitudes in the common soldiers, its higher ranks filled with men promoted from the ranks on grounds of "merit," and prepared to act, by its training, equipment, and discipline, in a great war among the old military powers of Europe. Eight marshals of Napoleon's empire, in addition to Bonaparte himself, were promoted to the rank of general officer at this time.

By spring of 1794 the French armies resumed the offensive. In June they won the battle of Fleurus, and the Austrians abandoned Belgium, In the Dutch cities the potential revolutionaries took hope again. The Poles, with Kosciuszko, again attempted revolution. Its outcome was uncertain. But in France it was clear, by mid-1794, that the Republic had survived.

It survived at a certain cost, or on certain terms. Much happened in France during the climactic Year Two of the republican calendar. Within the larger framework of the general eighteenth century revolution, and indeed of the subsequent history of modern times, it is illuminating to see two of these developments in some detail. First, the Revolutionary Government reacted strongly against popular and international revolution, exhibiting what, in the jargon, might be called "bourgeois" and "nationalist" inclinations. Second, in the extreme emotional stimulation, the Revolution, as understood by Robespierre, became the means to call a new world into being, and turned into something like a religion.

ALBERT GOODWIN (b. 1906) of the University of
Manchester was among the first to challenge the view
that the Directory was corrupt, inefficient, and
ineffective. In this article he argues that the Directory,
considering the obstacles before it, performed quite
well.*

Albert Goodwin

The Directory's Achievements

The French Executive Directory which
assumed office on 11 Brumaire year IV
(2 November 1795), and was destroyed by
Bonaparte's *coup d'état* of 18 Brumaire
year VIII (9 November 1799), has been
traditionally regarded by historians as
a byword for corruption, governmental
incompetence and political instability.
Its rule is usually associated with the
financial bankruptcy of 1797, defeats of
French armies in the field, administrative chaos at home and the Directors'
policy of self-perpetuation in office by
means of a series of "purifications" of the
elected Assemblies. In 1799 the Directory
is supposed to have been ripe for dissolution and France ready for Bonaparte.
It is the purpose of this paper to suggest
that such an interpretation does not do
full justice to the governmental record
of the Directory between 1795 and 1799,
and that it represents an over-simplification of the situation in France on the eve
of 18 Brumaire.

It is not difficult to see why, in the past,
the Directors have been so harshly
treated. The assumption that the Directors were themselves not exempt from the
vices of corruption and immorality char-
acteristic of French society at that date
was perhaps unavoidable, especially as
the Directory came to be identified in the
popular mind with Barras. This impression of Barras as representative of the
general standards of the Directory, although entirely erroneous, was to some

*Albert Goodwin, "The French Executive Directory—A Revaluation," in *History,* XXII, no. 87 (1937),
pp. 201–218. Footnotes omitted.

extent intelligible. Of the thirteen individuals who at various times held office as Directors, Barras alone succeeded in retaining his position throughout, and he was undoubtedly the most colourful personality of them all. The danger of generalising from the single case of Barras is, however, obvious. Another reason why injustice has been done to the Directory is that French history between 1795 and 1799 has tended to be studied by historians, very largely for the sake of convenience, as a period of *coups d'état.* This approach has had two unfortunate results. On the one hand, it has gained general acceptance for the impression that the age was one of perpetual crisis, thus distracting attention from the more solid achievements of the Directory, and, on the other, it has led to the supposition that it was this series of illegal expedients alone which ensured their survival. . . . Lastly, the reputation of the Directors may have suffered because it has been blackened by the apologists of Robespierre and the admirers of Bonaparte. Between Mathiez, who spent a lifetime in defending the Jacobin leader, and Madelin, equally intent on eulogising Bonaparte, the Directors have come in for a good deal of unmerited abuse. Few French historical scholars have been able to free themselves from partisanship in their accounts of the revolution, and the way in which the work of the Directory has been consistently underrated as a means of heightening the contrasts with the immediately preceding or following period is a good illustration of the evils implicit in such zeal. . . .

Shortly stated, the usual indictment may be said to be based on four main charges—that the personnel of the Directory was both corrupt and incapable; that its administration of the finances brought the country within measurable distance of ruin; that its foreign policy involved an indefinite postponement of the prospects of a general peace; and, finally, that the Government could not even fulfil the first condition of effective rule by securing public order and individual freedom at home. What modifications must be made in these charges in the light of the fuller evidence which is now available?

On the score of venality there is ample authority for the view that the Directors themselves were, with perhaps a single exception, reasonably honest. The corruption of Barras was, of course, notorious and remains indefensible. The evidence against the rest, however, is slight. Certain passages in Thibaudeau's Memoirs suggest that Reubell, who for some time virtually controlled Directorial finance, deserved censure, and some suspicion was apparently directed against Merlin de Douai and La Revellière. It is true that Reubell's reputation for financial integrity was not unblemished, since he had suffered disgrace for peculation under the Terror and he was well known to be avaricious. On the other hand, there is no real evidence against him of corruption while a Director, and it should also be remembered that the Commissions of Inquiry specially appointed by the Councils to investigate his guilt in August 1799 completely exonerated him as well as Merlin and La Revellière. When he retired from the Directory by lot on 16 May 1799, Reubell felt compelled to accept the allowance given by his colleagues as compensation, and he died poor. The rest of the Directors seem never to have been the objects of contemporary criticism on the ground of their dishonesty.

How far is it true to say that the Directors were individually men without ability? For the present purpose it is only necessary to consider the members of the original Directory and three others—François de Neufchâteau, Merlin de Douai and Treilhard. Sieyès may properly be excepted, as his efforts, after he became a Director, were concentrated on the destruction of the constitution of the year III. The others may be disregarded because of the shortness of their period of office—Barthélemy was in power three and a half months, Gohier less than six months, Ducos and Moulin four and a half months. The usual opinion of the original Directory—"les Pentarques"— is that they were a group of mediocrities. If only the highest standards are applied, such a judgment would not be unfair. But if the ordinary criteria of capacity are accepted, then the Directors must be credited with more than average ability. Mature they were bound to be since article 134 of the constitution insisted that they should be at least forty years of age, and although the manner of their nomination left something to be desired, they were all men of wide experience, most of them with special aptitudes and qualifications for the conduct of the departments of government they controlled. The least remarkable from the point of view of sheer ability were LeTourneur and Barras. Le Tourneur was entirely devoid of political gifts, and in all matters of policy he followed without question the lead of his school-friend Carnot. He did, however, possess a good knowledge of the technical side of naval affairs. The Directory needed a naval expert, and Le Tourneur admirably filled the gap. Similarly, it would be hard to think of any revolutionary leader, apart from Fouché, better fitted to organise the police than Barras, whose whole life had been spent in intrigue. Nor is it accurate to regard Barras as a political cipher. Especially when resolute action was needed, Barras could be counted on, as he had already shown on 9 Thermidor and 13 Vendémiaire. That he had an eye for talent as well as for beauty is proved by those whose careers he helped to make—Bonaparte and Talleyrand, Saint-Simon and Ouvrard. Luck alone cannot account for his survival till 18 Brumaire.

La Revellière was in many ways a curious mixture, half crank, half fanatic, a botanist, student of Rousseau, high priest of the new revolutionary cult of Theophilanthropy and a believer in the *juste milieu* in politics. A sincere republican, he was consumed with a hatred of priests and aristocrats, and yet he had small liking for the rural or urban proletariate. In foreign policy he was an advocate of the war of propaganda and conquest—an attitude which he had consistently maintained ever since the day he had been the prime mover of the decree of 19 November 1792 by which the Convention had promised its aid and protection to all nations who wished to recover their liberty. His special sphere in Directorial policy was education, the *fêtes nationales* and manufactures.

Carnot has been aptly described by Mathiez as "presque exclusivement un savant et un patriote." A former member of the Committee of Public Safety, and famous as the "Organiser of Victory," he had been nominated, in place of Sieyès, who had refused to serve as Director, in order to stem the run of French reverses on the Rhine. Carnot was a paragon of executive efficiency, and had real genius in the administration of war. He proved a failure as a Director, and for obvious reasons. He had a biting tongue and alienated his colleagues by his cynicisms. He was a convinced pacifist at a time when both Reubell and La Revellière, for different reasons, were keen supporters of foreign war. He disappointed the expectations of his Jacobin friends by evolving in the direction of the Right. Lastly, although he had little or no talent for politics, he was never satisfied to confine himself to his departmental duties. Still, he can hardly be described as a mediocrity.

There is general agreement that Reubell was a man of great ability. An Alsatian barrister of eminence, he had a good command of modern languages and an encyclopaedic knowledge. He owed his ascendancy over his colleagues to his industry and his strength of will. Utterly devoid of scruple and severely practical, he may be described as the main driving force behind Directorial policy. At one time he maintained a close supervision over the three most important departments of government—justice, finance and foreign affairs. Subsequently, however, he was content to delegate responsibility to ministers of proved capacity, such as Merlin and Ramel, and concentrated his own attention on the conduct of diplomatic affairs. In this sphere he identified himself with the policy of conquest and expansion which he hoped would culminate in the acquisition of the natural frontiers. As Reubell was only eliminated from the Directory by lot in May 1799, his influence upon policy was exerted throughout, and gave it a much-needed continuity.

Of François de Neufchâteau, Merlin and Treilhard, it is only necessary to say that the former was a distinguished administrator whose work as Minister of the Interior conferred lasting benefits on the French state and anticipated many of the Napoleonic reforms, and that Merlin and Treilhard were the leading jurisconsults of the day. Any government which could count on their services might well have considered itself fortunate.

The subject of Directorial finance is both technical and controversial. Here attention can only be directed towards one or two points which serve to modify the severe criticisms usually passed upon it. The two leading events upon which discussion has centred are the collapse of the Assignats in 1796 and the repudiation of two-thirds of the public debt in September 1797. Both these occurrences were, in some ways, regrettable, but, by themselves, do not entail an utter condemnation of the finance of the period. . . . The collapse of the Assignats prompted, it is true, an unsuccessful attempt to stabilise the paper currency by means of the *mandats territoriaux* in 1796, but this was followed by a return to a metallic currency without undue deflationary effects—a policy which may be said to have paved the way for that revival of confidence which is so often attributed to the Consulate. Similarly, the bankruptcy of 1797 should not be viewed in isolation, but be regarded as part and parcel of Ramel's economy campaign. Nor should it be overlooked that the bankruptcy itself was not only partial but conditional, and that the final blame for its becoming definite must rest with the Consulate. In fact, the suggested contrast between financial maladministration and chaos under the Directory and financial retrenchment and reform under the Consulate has no real relation to the facts, and should be abandoned. The foundation of the Bank of France in 1800 may have been symptomatic of a new regime, but it was only rendered possible by the financial reforms of the preceding period.

The immediate financial problem to be faced by the Directory was how to arrest the continued fall of the Assignats. One of the last acts of the Convention had been to establish by the law of 21 June 1795 a sliding scale of depreciation for contracts and other debts, the value of which was to be fixed according to the quantity of Assignats actually in circulation at the time of the signing of the contract. This experiment failed because it was not applied to all contracts and because the treasury had not a sufficient reserve. The first important proposal made by the Directory was for a forced loan payable in specie, corn, or in Assignats taken at 1 per cent. of their face value (6 December 1795). The manufacture of Assignats was to be discontinued and the plates broken on 21 March following. As the Assignats were worth less than 1 per cent. of their nominal value, and as receipts for payments of the forced loan were to be accepted in payment of direct taxes, this plan really amounted to a timid attempt at deflation and an effort to increase the revenue from taxation. The over-valuation of the Assignats and the lack of specie for their conversion, however, effectually ensured the failure of this scheme.

The next experiment—the issue on 18 March 1796 of *mandats territoriaux*—was devised by the Finance Minister, Ramel-Nogaret. These *mandats* were in effect a new form of paper money which it was hoped would gradually displace the Assignats and be immune from depreciation. To render them attractive to the public they were to entitle the holders to obtain *biens nationaux* at the fixed valuation of twenty-two years' purchase of the annual value of 1790. Unfortunately, however, a committee of the Council of Five Hundred made the Assignats convertible into *mandats territoriaux* at one-thirtieth of their nominal value. Thus, although the new facility provided for the acquisition of unsold national property prevented the *mandats* from depreciating immediately, they were bound to collapse eventually because of the over-valuation

of the Assignats in terms of the new paper-currency. It had been thought that the capitalists would eagerly take up the *mandats* in order to acquire the estates of the Belgian monasteries, but the more cautious of them hesitated to buy property so near to the frontier before the conclusion of a general peace, while the speculators preferred to discredit the *mandats* in order to effect purchases at a later stage at less cost. An additional difficulty was that the new currency was not immediately available, since the government only issued *promesses de mandats*. For these reasons the *mandats* failed to gain general acceptance, and despite the efforts of the government to force their currency, they quickly fell to a discount. In the course of July, August and September 1796 laws were passed whereby the *mandats* were to be accepted by the government in payment for taxes and in exchange for *biens nationaux* at their market price only. The *mandats* were finally withdrawn from circulation by a law of 4 February 1797. Thus failed the Directory's main effort at stabilisation. The failure was not, however, without its redeeming features, since it at all events prevented the inflation from getting completely out of hand, and it did in fact result in the resumption of a metallic standard.

In its essentials, the "repudiation" of 1797 was a comparatively simple operation. The law of 9 Vendémiaire year VI (30 September 1797) enacted that one-third only of the public debt should be consolidated and entered on the Grand Livre as a sacred charge, and that the capital of the other two-thirds should be redeemed by the issue to stockholders of bearer bonds *(bons des deux tiers mobilisés)*. By way of compensation, the state guaranteed that interest payments should in the future be made subject to no deductions as they had been in the past, and that the *bons des deux tiers* should be available for the purchase of national property.

It is clear that many of the contemporary arguments in support of the measure were either specious or merely absurd. Such, for example, was the suggestion that no injustice to fundholders would be involved, since their stock had already lost two thirds of its value owing to the inflation. Yet repudiation ignored the possibility of a recovery in the value of the public debt and made the former losses irretrievable. . . . Equally it must be admitted that the bankruptcy demolished the incomes of the rentier class. An example will suffice to show the extent of the injury and to elucidate the actual nature of the operation. A rentier with a capital of 3000 livres invested in the public debt which before September 1797 had given him, at 5 per cent., 150 livres interest, now received 50 livres as interest on one-third of his capital *(tiers consolidé)* and a nominal holding of 2000 livres in *bons des deux tiers mobilisés*. In the final liquidation of 30 Ventôse year IX (21 March 1801), when the two-thirds were converted into perpetual annuities at the rate of ¼ per cent. of their capital value, the 2000 livres would be exchanged for an annuity of 5 livres. The net result was that instead of receiving 150 livres interest, the fundholder received 55 livres, which meant that 63.34 per cent. of his capital had been destroyed. In this way the state repudiated in all nearly 2,000,000,000 livres of public debt. The consequent shock to public credit may be imagined. The spectre of national bankruptcy which had haunted Mirabeau in the early days of the revolution had at last materialised. . . .

It is, however, necessary to say in defence of the consolidation that bankruptcy in France had really been made inevitable by the misguided financial policy of the Constituent Assembly. The issue of the Assignats and the failure to levy sufficient taxation to balance the budgets had compromised the efforts of all subsequent administrations to grapple with financial shortage. The repudiation of 1797 was, in fact, only part of a larger scheme to effect reforms in the French budget. By reducing governmental expenditure from 1,000,000,000 to 616,000,000 livres, Ramel was able, for the first time in the history of revolutionary finance, to establish a balanced budget. Part of this economy was achieved by drastic reductions in the military estimates, but the main saving came from the consolidation of the public debt. The financial end in view was, therefore, sound enough in the circumstances, although the means were not. Finally, the responsibility for the final liquidation of 21 March 1801 must be borne by the Consulate. The real bankruptcy only came after the Directory had fallen.

One aspect of Directorial finance, also mainly due to Ramel, which deserves more general recognition, was the recasting of the whole system of direct and indirect taxation. . . . The new legislation relating to direct taxation was to be one of the most lasting achievements of the revolution, for it survived down to 1914. Some of it was fairly obviously a direct imitation of the younger Pitt's war finance, while the altered arrangements for the assessment and collection of revenue afford one more instance of a reorganisation the credit for which has been wrongly attributed to the Consulate. Finally, the fresh recourse to indirect taxation, itself a result of inflation, marked a significant reversal of the taxation policy of the early years of the revolution. The first direct tax to be reorganised was the tax on trade licences *(contribution des patentes)*. This had been re-established in 1795, not for fiscal purposes, but as a means of preventing unjustifiable trade practices. Some changes were introduced in the method of its assessment in 1796, and the final adjustments were made by the law of 22 October 1798. The land tax *(contribution foncière)* assumed definitive shape in the law of 23 November 1798, the new tax on doors and windows in that of 24 November. The latter duty, payable in the first case by the owner, but ultimately by the tenant, encountered considerable opposition, on the ground of its English origin. It may be regarded as a first approximation to an income tax, and the manner in which it was first doubled (1 March 1799) and then quadrupled (23 May 1799) as a means of meeting renewed war expenditure may be compared with Pitt's tripling of certain assessed taxes in 1797. Lastly, on 23 December 1798, the *contribution mobilière et personelle* which was partly a poll tax and partly a tax on movable property was entirely reconstructed. These four direct taxes (subsequently known as *les quatre vielles*) formed the essential structure of the French taxation system down to the outbreak of the World War. Equally important was the change instituted on 13 November 1798, whereby the assessment and collection of the direct taxes and the adjudications on appeals were removed from the hands of local elected bodies and entrusted to committees composed entirely of officials and working in the departments under the direct control of a commissioner of the central government. This fundamental reform was not inaugurated, but only continued by the Consulate. The only modification subsequently introduced was the change in the name of the officials.

Some of the features of the legislation on direct taxation reappeared in the revival of the indirect taxes. The very adoption of indirect taxation marked a reaction against the financial policy of the Constituent Assembly which had relied almost exclusively on direct taxes. Some of the new duties, such as the highway tolls, imposed on 10 September 1797, were again adopted from England. And hardly less permanent than *les quatre vielles* were the new mortgage, registration and stamp duties (November–December 1798). Other indirect taxes which proved indispensable were those on powder and saltpetre (30 August 1797), on gold and silver ornaments (9 November 1797), playing-cards (30 September 1798) and tobacco (22 November 1798).

A tendency to exaggerate the financial straits of the government may have inclined historians to accept with greater willingness Sorel's thesis that continued European war became a necessity to the Directors. The theory is at least plausible. On Sorel's view, war would ensure that the French armies would be occupied and prevented from interfering in politics at Paris, that the cost of clothing and feeding the troops would be borne by the foreigner, and that the empty coffers of the republic would be replenished by the confiscations and forced contributions levied on the conquered countries. Several unjustifiable assumptions have, however, to be made if this position is to be upheld. Sorel's assertion that France was "sans industrie, sans crédit, sans confidence" is demonstrably false. French industry might very well have absorbed the returned French armies—they need not necessarily have been put on half-pay. Nor should generalisations about the financial resources which the government drew from the activities of its armies abroad be accepted without caution. It requires to be proved that the war provided on balance a net income for the Directory. What figures we have point in the opposite direction. Moreover, if the main danger to the executive government was felt to be the existence of a class of ambitious generals, the real solution would have been not to prolong but to curtail the war, and thus to put an end to the extravagant pretensions and illicit gains of the commanders. There could be little doubt that the country as a whole wanted peace, and the Directors knew it. On *a priori* grounds, therefore, it is conceivable that the problems of peace confronting the Directory would not have been so insuperable as they have been made out.

Nor does the actual diplomacy of the period disprove the contention that the Directors were not averse from the conclusion of a satisfactory peace. The failure of the conference at Lille in July 1797, when Malmesbury had Pitt's instructions to spare no efforts for peace, was not entirely the result of the purge of the moderate party in the *coup d'état* of Fructidor or of the overbearing attitude of the Triumvirate. The breakdown must be placed at the door of Barras and Talleyrand, whose secret intrigues both before and after Fructidor did so much to prevent the English and French governments from reaching a frank understanding. Malmesbury at the outset agreed to the preliminary conditions put forward by the French agents. Recognition was given to the Republic, the annexation of Belgium and the French treaties of alliance with Holland and Spain. At the same time, however, he excepted secret

treaties and made no promise about a "general restoration" of conquered colonies. The French negotiators, Le Tourneur, former Director, Admiral Pléville Le Pelley and Maret, accepted Malmesbury's reservations, although these were quite inconsistent with the public articles of the Spanish treaty and the secret treaty with Holland. This initial ambiguity, with regard to the surrender of Dutch and Spanish colonies, was never explained to the Directory by its representatives. When, therefore, Malmesbury claimed the Cape and Ceylon, the Directory refused to consider his demands. Nevertheless, such was England's desire for peace that the government was even prepared to surrender the colonial conquests without compensation. Meanwhile, as the result of a ministerial reshuffle of 16 July, Talleyrand had become Foreign Minister. His English connections, his hopes of profitable speculative dealings on the London exchange and his sincere desire for peace all inclined Talleyrand to smooth away difficulties. He and Barras accordingly encouraged Pitt to believe that the French government, in return for hard cash, would not insist on the surrender of the Cape and Ceylon. Pitt consequently did not press the need for immediate concessions on his colleagues, and still reposed considerable faith in the prospects of the triumph of the moderates in Paris.

The precise effect of the *coup d'état* of 18 Fructidor upon the Lille conferences was that Le Tourneur, Maret and Colchen were replaced by Treilhard and Bonnier, who were instructed to present Malmesbury with a virtual ultimatum. It was to the effect that if he had not powers to cede all the English colonial conquests, he was to leave France, and not to return until he had. This new move, so far from being "a raising of the French terms," marked a reversion to the original demands. The Directory had not been informed that these conditions would be unacceptable from the British point of view, and it is clear that the Directors thought that Fructidor would enable them to impose this settlement. The ultimatum was conceived not as a means to end the peace negotiations, but as a way of exacting the full price from an enemy known to be in great difficulty. Malmesbury, having no authority to make the concessions, left Lille on 17 September with little or no hope of return. The resumption of negotiations was finally prevented by the battle of Camperdown. The Directory has always been strongly criticised by English historians for its failure to close with Pitt's offers, but the responsibility must not be borne entirely by the Directors. It was the secret intrigues of French agents at Lille which stiffened the English resistance before Fructidor, and which, after the *coup d'état,* were the cause of French intransigeance.

On the other hand, the approval which, under strong provocation from Bonaparte, the Directors gave to the preliminaries of Leoben and the final treaty of Campo Formio, cannot be regarded as indicative of the pacific views of the Directors. It is fairly certain that those treaties would have been rejected by the Directory if its hands had not been tied, and indeed the best interests of France demanded that Bonaparte's policy should have been set aside. The Directors had, in each case, ample room for dissatisfaction. At Leoben, Bonaparte, anxious to monopolise the credit of having concluded peace, speeded up negotiations in order to prevent the official French negotiator, General Clarke, from arriving in time to share the discussions. In the public articles of the preliminaries of peace

Bonaparte renounced the left bank of the Rhine, towards the acquisition of which Reubell's foreign policy had been mainly directed, and in the secret articles, by retaining the Duchy of Milan and suggesting the partition of Venice, he definitely disobeyed his instructions for the first time since the inception of the Italian campaign. In addition, it is clear that Bonaparte virtually conceded all that Thugut, the Austrian minister, wished to obtain. The principle of the integrity of the Empire was upheld, access to the Adriatic won, and the surrender by Austria of Belgium and Milan amply compensated for by her acquisition of part of Venice. When the articles of Leoben were read to them three of the Directors—Reubell, Barras and La Revellière—declared they were inacceptable, and the Minister for Foreign Affairs—Delacroix—also reported unfavourably on them. Yet on 30 April 1797 Reubell alone refused to sign the ratification of the preliminaries. The explanation must be sought in two ways—the Directors were compelled to accept Leoben because the French public, acquainted only with the public articles, had received the news with an enthusiasm which it would have been dangerous for the government to have damped, and, moreover, the rejection of the terms would have entailed an admission that Bonaparte's advance into Austria had in actual fact placed him in a very serious military position.

These incidents were paralleled by the negotiations at Campo Formio. Bonaparte withdrew from Austrian territory without waiting for the ratification of the Leoben preliminaries by his home government, and again ignored his instructions. He had been ordered by the Directors to renew the war rather than surrender Venice, and also to insist on the compensation of Austria in Germany. The actual terms of peace, however, conceded most of the advantages to Austria. As a result of the exchange of territory, her position was strengthened both in Italy and Germany, a check was placed on the ambitions of her rival Prussia, and she had the prospect of still further compensations if France succeeded in wresting the left bank of the Rhine from the representatives of the Empire in the projected congress at Rastadt. On the other hand, France deserted her ally Prussia, assumed a share of responsibility for the extinction of Venice, and erected in the Cisalpine Republic an uneasy neighbour whom it would be essential in the future to protect. Once more the Directors submitted, but most unwillingly. They could not afford to forfeit the position they had just won after Fructidor, nor did they wish to see a revival of the European coalition against France, as seemed not unlikely after the failure of the Lille conferences.

The net result of this double surrender on the part of the Directors was to deprive them of the initiative in French foreign policy and to substitute the Italian policy of Bonaparte for that of the natural frontiers as canvassed by Reubell. Moreover, in the years which followed Campo Formio the Directors did much successful work by assimilating the conquered territories in Belgium and on the left bank of the Rhine, by protecting the Italian republics and by exerting further pressure on Great Britain. In fact, for a whole year after Fructidor, French influence on the Continent was virtually unchallenged, and the real reverses suffered by French arms and diplomacy and the revival of the second Coalition must be ascribed not to Directorial incompetence, but to the initiation of the Egyptian expedition—a venture devised by Bonaparte and Talleyrand.

It is less easy to defend the inability of the Directors to secure internal peace and security. Here at least the record of the Directors was one of almost complete failure. This failure, however, only repeated the lapses of monarchical and previous revolutionary governments. Nor should it be overlooked that the task of maintaining public order in the provinces had become immeasurably more difficult under the Directory in consequence of the revival of royalism, the appearance of *chauffage,* and the adoption of conscription, (5 September 1798). Conscription was applied at an unfortunate moment—just at the time when the French armies had sustained a series of severe defeats and when the prospect of starvation was greater among the fighting forces than at home. Evasion of the law and desertion both helped to swell the number of brigands, who were able to organise "reigns of terror" in various parts of the country. It is customary to blame the government for having done nothing to face up to these difficulties. A long series of measures designed especially to grapple with brigandage, however, affords little support to this criticism. One of the first acts of the Directory after its acceptance of office was to add a seventh ministry—that of general police—to the six ministries provided for in the constitution, and to institute exhaustive inquiries into the state of the *garde nationale* and the gendarmerie. This investigation revealed defects which were, to some extent, remedied by a law of 17 April 1798 reforming the gendarmerie. Other administrative gaps were filled by the laws prescribing capital punishment for robbery with violence on the high roads and in private houses (15 May 1797), the law enforcing increased penalties against gaolers who connived at the escape of their prisoners (25 September 1797), and the law reforming the personnel of the criminal courts (10 January 1798). It must be admitted that these changes did not affect substantial improvement, but it is evident at least that the problem had been taken in hand. Above all, it should not be forgotten that in La Vendée, where political unrest had been so continuously dangerous to previous revolutionary governments, the problem may be said to have been solved by the Directory.

It only remains to summarise the reasons for thinking that the instability of the Directory has perhaps been exaggerated. This political insecurity has been ascribed partly to the Constitution of the year III, and partly to public hostility to the Directors and the general desire for a strong executive government on the eve of Brumaire. Further investigation, however, seems to be required before this line of argument can be regarded as satisfactory.

For, in the first case, there is something to be said for the view that the main constitutional difficulties of the Directors were in the course of time solved. The necessity of having a majority of at least three to two for the transaction of business may have opened the way to differences of opinion among the Directors, but after Fructidor (4 September 1797) the Triumvirate of Barras, Reubell and La Revellière removed this source of weakness. It was not until Reubell retired on 16 May 1799 and was replaced by Sieyès that this solidarity of the Directors was shaken. Similarly, the lack of any power to dissolve the Councils did not seriously hamper the Directors, since resort could always be had to systematic corruption at the annual election of one-third of the Councils or to a *coup d'état*. Although the right of initiating legislation lay with the Council of Five Hun-

dred, the Directors were not deprived of the power of giving effect to their policy, since the machinery of Directorial messages to the Legislative Assemblies proved an adequate substitute. Moreover, the formal absence of the power of initiation often provided the government with ready-made excuses when public opinion showed itself at all critical. Nor was the tenure of the Directory as a whole or of individual members of it really insecure. The life of the Directory was fixed at five years (Article 137)—a period which exceeded that of the Councils by two years and that of the Assemblies of 1791 and 1793 by three. As only one Director retired annually by lot, the political complexion of the executive could not be effectively altered by the Councils except after a wait of three years, and even then only on the unlikely assumption that the majority in the Councils remained stable. Finally, the substitution of three Consuls for five Directors at Brumaire left the form of the executive government very much the same.

Nor can French public opinion immediately before Brumaire be described as actively hostile to the Directors. The prevailing feeling was one of apathy rather than of antipathy. The initial reforming zeal of the revolutionaries had dwindled, people in the provinces had lost interest in electoral devices, and once the tide of victory against the foreigner had turned in favour of France the cry of *"La patrie en danger"* had lost its meaning. Now, in a situation of this kind the government in actual possession of power is not usually in a weak position, and it is doubtful whether in 1799 there was a general feeling in France that the overthrow of the Directory would do much to improve conditions. Hardly less widespread than apathy was fear—but this fear was of a peculiar kind: it was a fear of extremes, whether royalist or Jacobin. Fortunately for the Directors, the only formidable opposition to their rule came from precisely these two sources. For this reason the Directors had an easy means of prolonging themselves in office by *coups d'état* directed now against the Right, now against the Left. This *politique de bascule* far from being an indication of the essential instability of the government can be regarded as a source of strength. Not only was it effective, it was also consonant with the best interests of the country at large. As the representatives of moderate republicanism, the Directors could in this sense lay claim to a good deal of popular support.

Whether or not Frenchmen were willing on the eve of Brumaire to exchange the republican constitution of the year III for a military dictatorship cannot be decided with certainty. The difficulties encountered with the Council of Five Hundred at St. Cloud on 19 Brumaire, the cries of *"hors la loi"* which greeted Bonaparte and the well-known sympathies of the Parisian troops, at least make it clear that the constitution was still regarded as a bulwark against dictatorship. Bonaparte's military prestige had been somewhat tarnished by his abandonment of the army in Egypt and little was known of his political and administrative ability.

As a peacemaker, he still enjoyed the reputation he had gained at Leoben and Campo Formio, but Sieyès evidently thought that he would be willing to accept subordinate political office. Perhaps Vandal got nearest to the truth when he said of Bonaparte, "Il se laissait porter au pouvoir par un immense malentendu doublé d'un universel prestige." The theory of an "inevitable" military dictatorship has had a long innings; has not the time arrived when it should be abandoned? France in the autumn of 1799 was economically prosperous, the danger of invasion had already been averted, the reforms of Ramel and Neufchâteau were beginning to bear fruit, and the fear of reviving Jacobinism, dating back to the law of the hostages, might easily have been dealt with in the usual way. In religious matters it is difficult to believe the persecution of the priests was any more effective in practice than the measures taken to ensure public order, and although the desire for a restoration of the altars may have been pressing, there was considerable anxiety lest with it there should be associated a return of the church lands.

If Bonaparte had been forty instead of thirty, would he not have remained faithful to his original idea of becoming a Director?

JACQUES GODECHOT (b. 1907), a productive French scholar and professor at the University of Toulouse since 1945, has a broad range of interests. He has written an excellent book on civil-military relations during the period of the Directory and a volume on revolutionary and Napoleonic political institutions. He has also focused his attention upon the problem of the "Atlantic Revolution," and this selection presents his summary of non-French revolutions and their relationship to France.*

Jacques Godechot

World Revolution

The revolution gave way before the assault of the counterrevolutionary forces in the spring of 1799 and then rallied with such energy in the fall, because it possessed elements of both weakness and strength. We can identify these elements by examining the way in which the Atlantic world reacted to the revolutionary expansion. The essential agent of this expansion was France, the "Great Nation." This was what she came to be called both by admirers, who saw her as the great liberator of the peoples, and—in irony—by her deprecators, who thought she was driving the world to ruin. The Great Nation did not spread revolutionary ideas and institutions to the same extent everywhere. In the re-gions which France annexed, an attempt was made to implant them as strongly as at home. In the countries which were occupied but not annexed, the revolution developed in varying depths. The sister republics adopted constitutions and institutions which, though modeled on the French, nonetheless retained their originality. The other countries of Europe reacted to the revolution in diverse ways, depending on their social structure, their political position, and their geographical situation. Nor was the revolution confined to Europe. It was Atlantic in scope —Atlantic in the colonies of France, situated principally in the Antilles, which were thrown into confusion by the revolution; Atlantic too because of the in-

*Reprinted with permission of The Macmillan Company from *France and the Atlantic Revolution of the Eighteenth Century* by Jacques Godechot, translated by H. Rowen. Copyright © 1965 by The Free Press, a Division of The Macmillan Company. Pp. 207–229.

terest which not only the United States but also the Spanish and Portuguese colonies gave to the revolution in France. On the other hand, the revolution touched Africa only lightly, in the French occupation of Egypt, and Asia hardly at all, in the ephemeral French invasion of Syria and the agitation in the Mascarene islands and the French trading stations in India.

The Revolution in the Annexed Countries

France annexed the imperial principalities in Alsace and Lorraine (notably the principality of Salm), Avignon and Comtat-Venaissin, Nice, Savoy, the principality of Montbéliard, and the district of Porrentruy, by virtue of the "right of the peoples to self-determination." Some of these regions had been enclaves in French territory, and the existence of territories within France under foreign sovereignty shocked the rationality of those who had proclaimed the unity of the republic. It is beyond debate that the population in the enclaves were almost unanimous in their desire to join France. In all these districts the French language was spoken either by the entire population or at least by the bourgeoisie, so that revolutionary ideas had penetrated easily. Unlike the little enclaves, which not only did not offer any resistance to annexation but even welcomed it enthusiastically, Belgium reacted quite differently to this prospect. In 1792 Dumouriez, on the advice of Vonckist Patriots, had considered creating a Belgian republic similar to that which had been projected by the Belgians themselves in 1789. But at that time the Convention happened to be supporting the policy of "natural frontiers." On

December 15 it ordered the generals commanding the French forces in all the conquered countries to destroy the old regime, to replace the princely administrations by provisional governments "from which enemies of the republic shall be excluded," and then to have new governments elected, with all candidates required to take an oath "to be loyal to freedom and equality and to renounce privileges." In Belgium new communal and provincial assemblies were elected between January and March 1793. The majority were favorable to Belgian autonomy, and Dumouriez, who vaguely hoped to become the head of the new Belgian state, encouraged them to demonstrate these sentiments. He was going against the inclinations of the Convention, where Danton declared on January 31: "The limits of France are marked by nature. We shall attain them at the four corners of the horizon, at the Rhine, the ocean, and the Alps. That is where the boundaries of our republic must be." This implied the annexation of Belgium. Nonetheless, in the face of Belgian reluctance, it was felt to be too dangerous to hold either a general referendum or an assembly, as had been done in Savoy. Danton was sent on mission with other commissioners to obtain requests for annexation from local and provincial assemblies. The Convention decreed annexation of the different parts of Belgian territory by fifteen separate decrees between March 1 and 30, 1793. But by March 18 Dumouriez' army had been defeated and Belgium evacuated.

The Mountain, which came to power on June 2, 1793, did not favor the system of "natural frontiers." In any case it was not an immediate question, since France itself was being invaded. When after the victory of Fleurus French troops again penetrated into Belgium the Committee of Public Safety acted as if the annexations voted the previous year were null and void. Belgium was treated as a "conquered country" and given a provisional administration, which exploited it for the profit of France and the French armies, as if it would soon have to be abandoned.

The "natural frontiers" was proposed anew by the Girondin deputies who returned to the Convention in 1794 and gained increasing influence. The fate of Belgium was discussed during the first nine months of 1795. The partisans of the "lesser limits" policy opposed annexation, fearing that it would delay peace by making negotiations more difficult. Carnot advocated annexation only of a few fortresses. The supporters of the "natural frontiers" policy, after finally winning a majority in the Committee of Public Safety, triumphed in the Convention on October 1, 1795. There is a question nonetheless whether this vote was legally adequate to make Belgium a part of France, for the constitution of Year III specified that any annexation had to be ratified by the "French people." But the French people had already given their judgment upon the territorial limits of France by ratifying the constitution of Year III, which included the other annexations, but not that of Belgium which was never put to a specific referendum.

Even before the vote of October 1, 1795, Belgium was divided into nine departments, as well as cantons and communes, on August 31. After the annexation, a French commissioner, Bouteville-Dumetz, was instructed to promulgate the laws of France, which were introduced in Belgium between November 22, 1795, and January 20, 1797.

The adaptation of Belgium to the new regime was difficult, especially in the area of religion. The country was profoundly Catholic. Confiscation and sale of church property and the vexatious measures inflicted on the clergy angered the inhabitants. After the coup d'état of 18 Fructidor, the Directory ordered deportation of priests who refused the oath of "hatred for royalty and anarchy"; these included almost all the 8,200 Catholic priests in Belgium. Most went into hiding and escaped arrest, but two hundred were transported to French Guiana, where many died; several were sentenced to death and shot. The Belgian church became an unyielding enemy of the Directory.

Universal compulsory military service also met vigorous resistance. After the passage of the conscription law, which applied to Belgium, the peasants of Flanders and the Ardennes rose in rebellion, as the Vendeans had done in 1793. Lacking outside help, they were rapidly defeated.

It seems probable nonetheless that the petty bourgeoisie, who had profited by the sale of "national property" and obtained the majority of public offices, became satisfied with the new regime. Perhaps it was thanks to them that Belgium remained calm when the great counterrevolutionary thrust occurred in 1799. But this calm should not deceive us. Although many Belgians accepted the revolution, annexation to France was approved only by a minority. However, Austria officially ceded Belgium to France by the treaty of Campo Formio.

This treaty also included the annexation by France of the Ionian islands of Corfu, Cephallonia, and Zante, despoiled from the former republic of Venice. With their annexation the revolution reached into the Balkans world, but the penetration was merely superficial. The Ionian islands were divided into three departments, but the introduction of French institutions met resistance by the population, a majority of whom were Greeks in nationality and Orthodox in religion. In most cases it was not possible to hold elections; administrators and judges had to be named by the general who represented the French government. The French troops which landed at the end of June 1797 immediately began to levy requisitions and contributions. A general insurrection broke out when the Russian and Turkish ships appeared before the archipelago in October 1799. Yet it was through the Ionian islands that the revolutionary ideas penetrated into the Balkans. They were seeds that sprouted slowly, until they burst forth in the insurrection of Serbia in 1810 and Greece after 1820.

The last annexations accomplished by the Directory were those of Mülhausen on March 1, 1798, and Geneva, on April 15, 1799. Mülhausen was incorporated into the department of Haut-Rhin, within which it had enclaved. Geneva became the capital of a new department, Léman, formed from the territory of Geneva and part of Savoy. Mülhausen easily adopted French institutions, but not Geneva. The Genevans had been very proud of the independence of their little republic. They accepted incorporation into the Great Nation only with reluctance, and continued to miss their independence.

The Conquered Lands

There were also regions which were occupied by the French armies but not annexed. Their fate continued uncertain, but revolutionary ideas and institutions were introduced nonetheless. This occurred in the Rhineland, the island of Malta, and Egypt.

The French had broken into the Rhineland in the autumn of 1792, at the same time as into Belgium. The abolition of the old regime had been proclaimed but in general was not carried out in practice. The Patriots formed clubs, especially at Mainz. In March 1793, when the doctrine of the "natural frontiers" was approved by the Convention, the French government decided to have the local population vote upon annexation. As in Belgium, the vote was held in numerous local assemblies. A Rhenish Convention, elected by a tiny majority of the population, met at Mainz on March 21, 1793, and sent to Paris a request that France annex the Rhineland. But when the French troops were defeated in Belgium, they also withdrew from the Rhineland; Mainz soon came under siege and capitulated on July 23. The French did not return to the Rhineland until the summer of 1794, but they were not able to recapture Mainz; the Austrians held it until after the treaty of Campo Formio in December 1797.

Meanwhile those in the Convention who favored a "natural limits" policy demanded annexation of the Rhineland as well as of Belgium. Reubell, an Alsatian, was a particularly ardent advocate of annexation. The fact that the Rhinelanders spoke German would be no obstacle, he argued. The Alsatians spoke German too, and hadn't they been as good Frenchmen as any for a century and a half? He told the Convention how wealthy the Rhineland was—it was a major producer of coal, iron, and wool, it was well provided with modern ironworks and textile mills, and the best navigable waterway in Europe, the Rhine, ran along its eastern boundary. During the summer of 1795 a magazine at Reubell's suggestion instituted a prize competition on the question, "Is it in the interest of the French republic to extend its frontiers to the Rhine?" The supporters of annexation talked a great deal about prestige and power, but none of them mentioned the desires of the local population. Perhaps this is why the Convention decided not to take up the proposed annexation. When Reubell became a member of the Directory, he continued to push this policy. At his urging, Bonaparte was instructed to compel Austria to cede its territories in the Rhineland. We have seen that the general was satisfied with a vague promise by Austria, and that the Directory had to go along with him. The Congress of Rastadt was no more successful than Bonaparte in settling the question of the Rhineland.

The Rhenish Patriots and revolutionaries, fearing that French annexation of the Rhineland would not be achieved, still sought some way to avoid a return to the old regime. They proposed that an independent Cisrhenan republic be established in the Rhineland, on the model of the Cisalpine republic. General Hoche, who commanded the army of occupation, gave this proposal his approval and encouragement. After he died suddenly on September 19, 1797, the Directory, in which Reubell's influence had gone up after the coup d'état of 18 Fructidor, continued to take measures aimed at eventual annexation. Reubell obtained the appointment of his fellow-Alsatian Rudler to a position of control in the Rhineland in November 1797. Rudler divided the territory into four departments and gradually introduced French institutions. His measures against the feudal regime were even more radical than those adopted in France. All feudal dues and tithes were abolished without compensation. Land held on rental could also be acquired by the tenant on the basis of paying its worth—but he was required to reimburse the landowner only if the latter could show an original deed of leasehold untainted by any feudal dues.

The abolition of feudalism proved to be permanent. None of the governments which ruled the Rhineland after 1798 dared to reverse these measures. They made the peasants a satisfied class, which generally remained calm during the great offensive of the allies against France in 1799. Juridically, however, the Rhineland remained a part of the Holy Roman (German) Empire.

Malta at this period also was an occupied but not annexed country. The island's strategic position was of the first importance in the Mediterranean. As soon as French forces occupied the Ionian islands, Bonaparte planned to seize Malta from the Knights of St. John of Jerusalem. The island was poorly defended and it was easily taken by the French on June 12, 1798. Before leaving for Egypt, Bonaparte organized Malta "in the French manner," with municipalities, cantons, and a top administration of nine members. But the question of annexation by France was submitted neither to the French legislative councils nor to the population of the island. In any case the inhabitants, angry over the requisitions and the taxation which rained down on them, revolted on September 2. The English and the Sicilians, who were the masters of the sea after the disaster of the French fleet at Abukir (August 1), supported the rebels, who drove out the French. Nonetheless, the French occupation left its traces in Malta. Return of the Order of St. John became impossible, and the idea of independence remained to ferment.

The temporary French occupation of Egypt was of enduring importance, for it was through Egypt that the revolution reached Africa and the borders of Asia. After destroying the feudal regime of the Mameluks, who had ruled the country, Bonaparte was in a position to liberate the Egyptian people. Instead he continued the harsh subjugation of the *fellahin* to the traditional hierarchies, which he brought under French control. But in breaking the bond that united Egypt to the Ottoman Empire for three hundred years without interruption, Bonaparte—and with him revolutionary France—acted as precursors of Egyptian independence. The principal French effort was to modernize and rationalize the administration of Egypt. At the head of each of the provinces were placed an *aga*, the chief police, and an intendant, who directed the financial services: they were assisted by a *divan,* or council of seven members, which remained closely supervised by a French general and a French commissioner. At the head of the administration of the country Bonaparte placed a general divan of thirty Egyptian notables, which had only a consultative role. This organization of the Egyptian government was an innovation of fundamental significance. It meant the penetration of the Enlightenment into the Near East, the crossroads of Africa and Asia, where for three centuries there had seemed to be no change. Yet the old taxes were maintained, and in the judicial field the French confined themselves to creating two commerical tribunals. Bonaparte was insistent upon respecting freedom of religion. He proclaimed his personal sympathy for Islam. The first modern hospitals were created for the army; the doctors who accompanied the expedition began the study of tropical diseases and their cure. Did Bonaparte intend to make Egypt a French colony to replace Santo Domingo, where the plantations had been destroyed by the slave revolt? Or did he wish only to make Egypt a modern state which would awaken the Middle East under the influence of France? It is difficult to say what he really intended, but it is incontestable that the French revolution lies at the origin of the transformations which took place first in Egypt and then in all the Arab countries.

The Sister Republics

The establishment of free independent "sister republics" was part of the general conception of a great revolution to liberate all peoples. Anacharsis Cloots, a German refugee in France, and some French revolutionaries, particularly the Girondins, dreamed of a world federation of equal republics, but they had only sketchy notions of how to achieve it. The creation of new republics was the work of France, the Great Nation, thanks to its military victories. The new republics, which were small, weak, and always in danger from powerful neighboring states where the old regime still held sway, could not survive without the help of France. In fact, therefore, they were less sister republics than vassal states. Furthermore, the Directory was more interested in territorial expansion than in more control. For reasons of both domestic and foreign policy, as we shall see, the Directory opposed the formation of the unified republic in Italy, which some Patriots in the peninsula already advocated. The policy of creating sister republics, therefore, did not succeed, but it had great consequences nonetheless, for it carried the French doctrines, ideas, and institutions to the Low Countries, Italy, and Switzerland and made the revolution in these countries an integral part of the Revolution of the West.

Leaving out of consideration the ephemeral Rauracian republic, which was established in 1792 in Porrentruy and was annexed to France on March 23, 1793, there were six sister republics: the Batavian, recognized by France in the treaty of The Hague of May 16,1795; the Cisalpine, recognized by Austria in the treaty of Campo Formio of October 18, 1797; the Ligurian, formed from the previous republic of Genoa on June 6, 1797; the Roman, proclaimed February 15, 1798; the Neapolitan (Parthenopean), created January 26, 1799; and the Helvetic, organized in April 1798. Three other attempts at creating such regimes failed. After the entry of French troops into Venice in April 1797, the city was "democratized," but it had to be ceded to Austria six months later by the treaty of Campo Formio. After the king of Sardinia was driven out by the French in December 1798, the Piedmontese Patriots hoped to make their country a republic, but the Directory decided to hold a referendum in Piedmont on annexation by France. This vote was held on February 16, 1799, under dubious conditions, and the annexation was approved. Finally, when the French entered Tuscany after the departure of the grand duke in March 1799, they prepared to organize a republic, but they had to leave the country in late April before the new regime was proclaimed.

The first thing the sister republics did on coming to power was to write constitutions. These were all inspired by the French constitution of Year III; this is not surprising, for France was the Great Nation, the propagator of the revolution which was to bring happiness to the peoples. Nonetheless, with rare exceptions, these constitutions were not servile copies of their French model. Sometimes they took inspiration from articles in the French constitution of 1793; more often they took into account local aspirations and the reforms which their own jurists had already proposed. Holland, Switzerland, and Tuscany had all experienced

important movements of study of public law reform. It should not be forgotten that Tuscany had almost been the first country in Europe to have a modern constitution. Drawn up by the philosophers Gianni, Paolini, and Tolomei, it was set aside by Grand Duke Peter Leopold only because of the formal objections of his brother, Emperor Joseph II, who feared that it would cause a revolution.

Several of the new constitutions were adopted after they had been submitted to a popular referendum. This was the case with the Batavian constitution. A first draft was rejected on August 8, 1797, by a coalition of Right and Left; the conservatives felt that it was too revolutionary and the democrats that it was too moderate. This was the second time during the eighteenth century that a constitution had been rejected by the people anywhere in the world; the first time had been in Massachusetts in 1778. Another constitution was drafted which was closer to the French constitution of Year III than its predecessor. It was adopted in the referendum of April 23, 1798, by 154,000 votes to 11,600. In Italy the constitution of the Cisalpine republic was drawn up by a committee of Italian jurists and politicians. They borrowed numerous articles from the constitutions of the ephemeral Bolognese and Cispadane republics established in late 1796 and early 1797, which had been widely discussed by fairly representative elective assemblies. The constitution of the Ligurian republic was written by a legislative committee and approved in the referendum of December 2, 1797, by 100,000 votes to 17,000. The Neapolitan constitution was also the work of local Patriots. On the other hand, the constitution of the Roman republic was written by French commissioners and reproduces the constitution of Year III, sometimes word for word. However, it gave the French institutions names borrowed from Roman antiquity; there were consuls instead of directors, praetors instead of judges, and so on.

The Helvetic constitution was drafted by the Basel patriot Peter Ochs, but was revised by the French Directors Reubell and Merlin of Douai. It was submitted to a referendum; some cantons endorsed it by large majorities, others rejected it, and some even rebelled against it. The four "Original" cantons and the Valais did not accept it until they had been defeated by French troops in bloody combat.

All these constitutions created unified and centralized states; they gave power to the bourgeoisie on a more or less wide basis of property qualification, different in each republic; suffrage was universal in the Batavian, Helvetic, and Cisalpine republics. All proclaimed freedom and equality of rights. They abolished the seignorial regime under conditions which varied according to the country. They suppressed the nobility and the privileges of the clergy; they often (but not always) abolished the guilds and their component institutions. The relations of religion and the state, which had so gravely troubled France, were the subject of careful study, and everywhere care was taken to avoid schism. The Ligurian republic recognized Catholicism as the state religion. In general, these constitutions borrowed the notion of social rights from the French constitution of 1793 to a greater degree than did the French constitution of Year III. The Batavian constitution proclaimed that the laws should provide for improvement of public health and that the state should furnish "work to the industrious and assistance to the poor." The Ligurian constitution affirmed that "society owes the means of subsistence to the indigent and education to all citizens." The Neapolitan constitution declared that a citizen has the duty of helping his fellow men, feeding the indigent, and enlightening and instructing those around him. The control of the central government over provincial administrations was better organized in Helvetia and the Roman republic, where appointed prefects directed the administration of each department, than it was in France. In the Neapolitan republic provision was made for a kind of constitutional court, an "assembly of ephors," to sit fifteen days each year for the purpose of determining whether the constitution had been violated during the preceding year. The French constitution of Year VIII was inspired by these institutions.

Although the Patriots were a minority in all these republics, the new institutions might have functioned normally if the French government had not constantly interfered in local politics through its commissioners and ambassadors. The French Directory was in fact fearful that power would be seized by the more democratic Patriots, whom it looked on as "anarchists." It suspected—with good cause—that they were in contact with Babeuf, Buonarroti, and their friends and drew inspiration from their doctrines. The Directory endeavored to destroy the influence of the advanced democrats. It was equally hostile to the moderates, whom it suspected of wishing to re-establish the old regimes. The French Directory was therefore led to maintain in power men on whom it believed it could count but who were often only puppets without influence in their own countries.

When the Batavian and Cisalpine republics were established in 1796 and 1797, the moderates who had been in control of French policy since the discovery of the Babeuf conspiracy favored as rulers in these two states men whose opinions were as neutral as possible. But the Jacobins, who returned to power in France after the coup d'état of 18 Fructidor Year V (September 4, 1797), considered it indispensable to "democratize" the sister republics. In the Batavian republic, General Joubert, helped by the Dutch general, Daendels, arrested the federalist deputies on January 22, 1798; they had opposed the introduction of a more centralized and more democratic regime, which the Patriots demanded. In the Cisalpine republic General Brune forced three Directors to resign (April 13, 1798), also at the suggestion of local Patriots. In the Helvetic republic, army commissioner Rapinat called upon two moderate Directors to resign and brought the Jacobin Peter Ochs into the Directory.

But the wind had already turned in France. The Directory, which invalidated the election of Jacobin deputies by the coup d'état of Floréal Year VI (May 11, 1798), also desired to be rid of their friends, the Jacobins in power in the sister republics. This was the source of a new series of coups d'état. In the Batavian republic, General Joubert, again with the help of Daendels, arrested a Batavian Director and several deputies upon the orders of the Directory in Paris; two other Dutch Directors had to resign and the municipal governments of Amsterdam and Rotterdam were dismissed. In the Cisalpine republic, the Jacobins who had come to power several months before were expelled on August 30 and December 10, 1798. A new constitution which repealed universal suffrage and in general was less democratic than the constitution which had been in force was introduced by the French minister at Milan, Trouvé.

The formation of the Second Coalition and the sharpening of the counter-revolutionary threat led to election of numerous Jacobin candidates in the French elections of early 1799. They gave their support to the Batavian and Neapolitan Jacobins, whose influence rose. However, the successes of the coalition prevented any further increase in the power of the Jacobins in the sister republics. In fact, the Cisalpine republic, invaded by the Austrians and Russians, collapsed in April 1799. The Neapolitan and Roman republics were the prey of counterrevolutionary insurrections as soon as the French troops marched out. The governments retained no authority outside Naples and Rome, the capitals. The Batavian, Ligurian, and Helvetic republics became the theater of major military operations. The republican institutions, which in these countries rested upon old traditions, survived, but all power passed to French generals.

The Revolution in Europe

The revolutionary movement made continuous progress in Europe until around 1793 or 1794. Thereafter it began to retreat wherever there were no French armies in occupation. The established governments had become cognizant of the revolutionary danger. The war against France strengthened their authority and their means of action. The organization of the counterrevolution improved and it acquired a doctrine. A hunt for Jacobins began. Revolutionaries were tracked down and their societies dissolved. Their plots were betrayed by informers and the members of their clubs were tried and punished.

As we have seen, it was Great Britain where the revolutionary movement undeniably had acquired the greatest breadth outside France. It was there, too, that it met its most categorical reply at the level of doctrine, in Burke's *Reflections on the Revolution in France* — a book that detached an important fraction of the British bourgeoisie from the revolution. In any case, the interests of English businessmen were threatened when the French occupied Antwerp at the end of 1792 and reopened the Scheldt river to shipping. The English bourgeoisie accepted the war against France without protest, and the war enabled the government, led by the younger Pitt, to sharpen its measures against the revolutionaries. Their clubs were closed; agitators and writers who supported the French revolution were brought to trial before carefully selected juries and given harsh sentences. After Parliament granted Pitt's request for suspension of the Habeas Corpus Act on May 16, 1794, suspects were arbitrarily arrested and enrolled as seamen in the Royal Navy.

But disorders and disturbances among the people continued. They were spurred by French victories in 1795, which inflicted serious damage on British trade, and by the short harvests of 1794 and 1795, which caused a rise in the price of food. Rioting broke out in London, Birmingham, and Dundee. When Parliament met on October 27, 1795, King George III and Pitt were violently attacked during the course of a public meeting. The government replied by sharpening its repressive measures. Meetings of more than fifty persons were forbidden except in the presence of a magistrate. Seditious publications were prosecuted. At the same time, however, steps were taken to reduce the price of bread. The crisis eased. Agitation fell off, at least in England proper, but it persisted in secret in Ireland and among the sailors of the fleet.

On April 15, 1797, a mutiny shook the Channel fleet based at Spithead. Richard Parker, a sailor, proclaimed a "floating republic" in the North Sea fleet when it also mutinied, on May 11. Negotiations between the Admiralty and the mutineers led to the capitulation of the Channel squadron; the North Sea fleet then had to give in too. Parker was tried and hung. A French landing in England might well have succeeded if the French government had taken advantage of these mutinies, which immobilized the British navy. It seems probable that the mutineers had connections with French Jacobins, but they were linked principally with the Irish secret societies, particularly the United Irishmen.

Secret agitation in Ireland had continued after 1780. In an effort to restore calm, Pitt granted the vote to Catholics, but it was inadequate — the Irish Catholics demanded complete equality with Protestants. The Whigs in Pitt's cabinet were inclined to concede such equality as well, but George III was opposed to it and Pitt accepted the king's decision. Disorders increased in Ireland, sustained by the Society of United Irishmen under the leadership of Wolfe Tone. In Ulster the United Irishmen organized an outright civil war and sought help from France and the United States. In late December 1796 the French sent an expeditionary force under the command of Hoche to land in Ireland. An error in tactics caused their fleet to be divided into two groups as soon as it left Brest. Only a few French ships reached Ireland, and the landing could not be made. Nevertheless the revolutionary agitation in Ireland continued, encouraged by the mutiny of the British fleet in the spring of 1797. A general rebellion broke out in Ireland early in 1798. It was a vast peasant insurrection, similar to the revolt of the Vendée in

France. But the French were not then ready to send help to the Irish. They did send a small squadron in August 1798, but more to create a diversion for the sake of their own Egyptian expedition than to support the Irish rebels. General Humbert, who landed with a French half-brigade on August 22 at Killala Bay, was able to rally only a few peasants. He ventured nonetheless to within sixty miles of Dublin, but his force was trapped and he had to surrender to the British on September 8. Wolfe Tone was captured aboard a French ship and committed suicide while in prison. The suppression of the Irish rebellion was very harsh; more than 30,000 victims were reported. England treated Ireland as a conquered country. The Act of Union of 1800 proclaimed that Ireland was indissolubly tied to Great Britain; it lost its own parliament, and the Catholics were deprived of the few rights they had possessed.

The revolution in Great Britain was defeated for a long time—but it had been a close call. In recalling these events, we can understand the stubbornness of the English government in its war with France. In struggling against revolutionary France, it was also combating the development of the revolution in Great Britain itself.

These revolutionary troubles also explain both the peace initiatives of the English government and their failure. Pitt wished to negotiate only with a French government that would repudiate all revolutionary propaganda. He consented to enter negotiations through Lord Malmesbury in October 1796, when, after the discovery of the Babeuf plot, the moderates were in power in France. These negotiations failed as the result of the demands of the English, who were willing to recognize only France's bound-

aries of 1792 plus Nice and Savoy, and demanded for themselves cession of the Dutch overseas possessions of the Cape Colony and Ceylon. The negotiations resumed at Lille on July 7, 1797, still with Lord Malmesbury as intermediary; the partial elections for the legislative councils in France (one-third of the membership had to be renewed annually) brought a triumph of the Clichyans. The negotiations were broken off immediately after the coup d'état of 18 Fructidor, which returned Jacobins to power. It was feared that establishment of peace and the resulting easy communications with France would greatly increase the peril from the revolutionary danger in Ireland, then growing rapidly. The need to combat the revolution within its own territory held a top priority in the entire policy of Great Britain from 1793 to 1799. In forming the second coalition cabinet against France late in 1798, Great Britain proved that it was the soul of the counterrevolution.

In Germany the revolution caused less serious problems than in England. By 1794 the conspiracies of the Austrian and Hungarian Jacobins had been uncovered and their leaders condemned to death and executed. The policy of the Hapsburgs became one of violent reaction. All partisans of the Enlightenment were dismissed from public office—although the two predecessors of Francis II had chosen their principal councilors from among them. All societies were put under close surveillance and student associations were dissolved. The police became all-powerful, opening letters, raiding homes, and controlling the press. Sale of the works of the philosopher Kant was banned. Still the liberals continued to have some supporters at court; under their pressure Thugut, the minister of foreign affairs, began preliminary negotiations with France at Basel in June and July 1796. These were broken off for a while when the Austrian troops won some victories in Germany. But, after Bonaparte won his triumphs in Italy, the liberals compelled Thugut to sign the preliminary peace of Leoben on April 18, 1797. The counterrevolutionary action bore fruit when, on April 15, 1798, a popular riot took place against the embassy of France in Vienna because the republican shield had been attached to the balcony and the tricolor flag had been raised.

In the other states of Germany a reaction modeled upon the repression in Austria raged. In Bavaria Jacobins were accused of treason and brought to trial. In the small states of central Germany, writers ceased to publish work favorable to the revolution; Goethe and Schiller kept silence. In Prussia Sieyès, who had been sent by the Directory as the ambassador of France, was given a glacial reception in June 1798.

Eastern Europe was shut off more tightly than ever from revolutionary influences. Police terror reigned in Poland after the third partition (1795). In Russia a number of peasant insurrections broke out between 1796 and 1798; the nobility blamed the rebellions—without justification—upon the influence of the French revolution, and abandoned whatever sympathy they had shown for it. Tsarina Catherine II, who died on November 7, 1796, was succeeded by her son Paul I, a person of impulsive and abnormal character. He was so opposed to the French revolution that he forbade use of the words "citizen," "fatherland," "freedom," and "constitution." Paul I

was one of the principal animators of the second coalition and the Russian army and navy took an active part in the war against France.

In Scandinavia, the kingdoms of Sweden and Denmark endeavored to maintain their neutrality. King Gustavus IV Adolphus, who succeeded the assassinated Gustavus III in Sweden, had difficulty in establishing his authority and did not summon the Riksdag until 1800. In Denmark the leading minister Bernstorff attempted to mediate in 1797 between France and England to restore peace. After he failed, he became the most zealous defender of the neutrality of the Scandinavian states.

In the Balkans, after Turkey declared war on France in 1798, it resisted the penetration of revolutionary ideas with increased vigor. Rhigas and eight of his friends who were turned over to the Turks by the Austrians were strangled in a Belgrade prison. Spain and Portugal, which were at peace with France, could not show as much severity, but the still powerful Inquisition prevented the importation of French books and newspapers; even French priests who had emigrated to Spain were subjected to very strict conditions of residence. The revolutionary propaganda had no success in the Iberian peninsula.

By the beginning of 1799 the revolution had found its limits in Europe—the Rhine, the Alps, and the eastern coast of the Adriatic. It affected primarily the Atlantic countries, with the exception of Spain and Portugal. But the revolution did not halt at the shores of the Atlantic; it crossed the ocean and had a profound effect in America.

FRANKLIN L. FORD (b. 1920), a historian at Harvard
University, has done research on the structure of the
French nobility during the Old Regime and on the
nature of urban life in eighteenth-century Strasbourg.
In this selection, taken from an article dealing with
the impact of the French Revolution, he presents his
interpretation of the effect of the upheaval on French
and European society.*

Franklin L. Ford

The Revolution:

Continuity or Change?

Every student of history, regardless of his special field, faces a problem of choice, endlessly recurring but constantly recast. Put in terms that seem to us worn only because none of us can wholly avoid using them, the choice is between emphasis on continuity and emphasis on change. No matter how he may hedge or qualify, the historian, before he completes an investigation, must respond to the question Carl Becker used to ask his seminar at Cornell: "Should we finally insist that while the world may change, it changes slowly— or that while the world may change slowly, it does change?" Everything in our professional training supports the first proposition, yet our fascination with historical process would forsake us if we did not also believe the second.

Actually, of course, real sophistication implies an ability to keep both tendencies in view, to exploit within our own minds the dialectic between solid evidence of continuity and unblinkable signs of change. It is equally clear that one may tip the balance this way or that in his analysis of a particular situation without thereby assuming a rigid posture in defense either of change or of continuity as the key to all understanding of the past. . . .

A number of powerful arguments have been leveled against the view . . . that in the years after 1789 an older Europe collapsed and that a new one, ominous in its strangeness, came into being. Various scholars have warned us that to interpret the revolutionary-Napoleonic

*Franklin L. Ford, "The Revolutionary-Napoleonic Era; How Much of a Watershed?" in *American Historical Review*, LXIX, no. 1 (1963), pp. 18–29. Footnotes omitted.

era as a chasm over which no one could cross from the eighteenth century into the nineteenth, or as a wall of flame through which nothing could pass intact, would be to distort reality beyond recognition.

Against even the more modest image of a revolutionary "watershed" the arguments are impressive. They are also, in my view, an essential antidote to the kind of oversimplification to which such an image may lend itself. . . .

As most commonly formulated, this case rests on the assertion that it was the seventeenth century, sometimes extended to include the first years of the eighteenth, which saw the fundamental break between an old and a "modern" Europe. Once this great change in both ideas and institutions had occurred, so runs the argument, there ensued a period extending into the early twentieth century, a period best envisaged as a plateau, marked by hummocks and creek beds, but never divided by a major watershed. Specifically, the revolutionary-Napoleonic interlude appears to shrink to the dimensions of an overrated episode the dust from which, once it settled, proved to have been just that—dust, having no deep significance for the substratum of continuity in human affairs. . . .

Perhaps the earliest argument for continuity was published by Albert Sorel almost eighty years ago in the first volume of his *L'Europe et la Révolution française,* which stressed the tenacious ambitions governing the intercourse of sovereign states from the eighteenth century through the revolutionary age. Readers of John U. Nef's *War and Human Progress* will recall his rejection of the older, more cataclysmic vision of an "Industrial Revolution." According to Nef, the crucial economic changes by which Europe and the rest of the world have indeed been revolutionized cannot

be assigned to the years 1760–1832. . . . Rather, those changes may be seen in the offing by the mid-seventeenth century, accelerating unevenly both in England and in France during the eighteenth, reaching literally earth-shaking intensity in Germany and the United States by the mid-nineteenth. . . .

It seems to me to have been demonstrated beyond question that the development both of ideas and of institutions from what most of us still call early modern into modern times must today be discussed, if not in terms of flat continuity, at least in terms of complex, irregular, and in some areas exceedingly slow change. The influence of this demonstration on historical thinking has been reinforced, as earlier noted, by examples of both the eighteenth century's foreshadowing the nineteenth, and the latter's turning backward toward the former. We have been warned, for instance, that the preconditions for an outburst of popular nationalism existed long before that force was unleashed by revolutionary France. We have been reminded that Rousseau, Diderot, and the young Germans of the *Sturm und Drang* in the 1770's adumbrated many of the characteristics of later romanticism. Looking in the opposite direction, we have had to examine the revival of ecclesiastical power after the long humiliation of the papacy, a revival symbolized in 1814 by the rehabilitation of the Society of Jesus. In a different quarter, we have been shown how many of the administrative and social changes launched by the Prussian reformers of Baron vom Stein's era had been undone by 1819 at the latest. Finally, we reflect that the dynastic principle, challenged by mobs and by political theorists, perverted by a Corsican family's willingness to serve, was in 1815 firmly reasserted in France, Spain, and the Italian principalities, extended to the Netherlands, and given new scope in the kingdoms and grand duchies of southern Germany.

Taken by themselves, all these affirmations and reminders seem to leave us no choice but to abandon the conception of a revolutionary-Napoleonic "watershed." . . . It is just at this point however, that I must define a view which will be developed in the remainder of these remarks, for I believe that it is not enough simply to recognize important strands of continuity linking the eighteenth century to the period that followed. When all due attention has been paid to those strands . . . it still is not clear that we must slide into suggesting to ourselves, our readers, or our students that the revolutionary-Napoleonic era really did not make much difference. On the contrary, it is time again to emphasize certain changes witnessed by that era, changes so fundamental that no historian can move from eighteenth- to nineteenth-century subject matter without major adjustments in his conception of Europe and in the terms he must use. It is time to say, if I may in a sense use Alfred Cobban's phrase against him, that the Revolution was no "myth." . . .

There are several quite different types of evidence to which we might usefully address ourselves. Who can deny, for example, that nearly every major European government came out of the revolutionary-Napoleonic crisis with its administrative organization profoundly and, as time was to show, irreversibly altered? After 1815 France retained a set of budgetary procedures, a network of departmental prefects, and a system of centrally appointed judges in place of the deficit financing ex post facto, the quaint chaos of provincial powers, and the court system based on ownership of office with which the old monarchy had lived for

centuries. But it was not only the brilliant and terrible homeland of the Revolution that changed its methods of conducting governmental business. The administrations of other states, hostile to France but stunned by its success in mobilizing national resources moved toward lasting reforms through what might be termed "defensive modernization." I shall here mention just three imposing examples: the British income tax, begun by William Pitt in 1799, revamped by Henry Addington in 1803; the establishment of the Prussian Ministry of War, the Great General Staff, and the Military Academy by Gerhard von Scharnhorst and his collaborators after 1807; and the creation in 1802 of central ministries even for stubborn Russia. However the governments of Europe may be characterized after the Congress of Vienna, they cannot be dismissed as mere survivals of the *ancien régime.*

A second set of changes took place in the nature of warfare, going far beyond the reorganization of military command functions and training, just mentioned in the case of Prussia. What happened over the twenty-three years between Valmy and Waterloo, the years of Marengo and Trafalgar, Austerlitz and Borodino, was a revolution in the demands, the implications, the very sociology of war. . . . Here again, the continental enemies of France had to imitate or perish. By the time Napoleon was at last defeated, Europeans had experienced, if not total war, at least their first taste of what total war, including economic warfare, might be like under modern conditions.

The broadening and intensification of conflict were only the most obvious symptoms of a third type of change. This was the increased public involvement in politics. It was not just a matter of patriotism. Behind the sharp call of duty to the fatherland in danger, to the *patrie* as it was coming to be understood, could be heard a rising chorus of insistence on political rights for more citizens, though nowhere yet for all citizens. Palmer, in the study already noted, has shown that even before 1789 this insistence had been so clearly heard, and so strongly resisted by privileged groups, that the great crisis both inside and outside France was in part a "reaction against reaction." It was the Revolution itself, nevertheless, which mounted the most sweeping demands that, somehow, the people's representatives must be heard. Napoleon, while he subverted that demand, paid it lip service. After his fall, the restored dynastics compromised with it where necessary and condemned it where possible. If, however, it had subsided after 1815 like the winds of a passing storm, historians would not speak of the era of repression as essentially an episode. Instead, they could describe a lasting resumption or aristocratic "normalcy" drawn to the specifications of Friedrich von Gentz and Prince Metternich.

Still a fourth level of revolutionary change belongs to the realm of literature, music, and the visual arts. When dealing with the communication of sentiments, of course, we can scarcely expect to emerge with anything more tangible than an awareness of altered tone, an impression of changed intensity. . . . How can we in turn . . . escape a powerful sense of change . . . of heightened emotional temperature, of art struggling to express newly unleashed passions when we contrast Pope with Shelley, Mozart with Berlioz (or even the Beethoven of the later symphonies), Goya of the court portraits and the tapestry cartoons with him of the "Horrors of War"? Must we not acknowledge that the differences represent long strides away from the sometimes cold confidence of the eighteenth century in *la raison raisonnante?* . . .

Having said this much, let me now state my own conviction that nowhere —neither in administrative innovations, nor in the altered conditions of war, nor in the first uneven surge toward political democracy, nor in the highly charged cultural atmosphere—do we perceive at its clearest the fundamental shift that makes the last years of the eighteenth century and the first of the nineteenth a historical watershed too imposing to be disregarded. The most important change of all occurred in social structure and, equally important, in the way men conceived of social structure. We need above all to consider what it meant for European society to lose the appearance of a hierarchy of legally defined orders of men. By the same token, we must consider what it meant to have nakedly revealed the social subdivisions identified by Max Weber in a famous and by no means outdated essay: classes, as economic groupings; status groups, reflecting degrees of honorific recognition; and parties, organized around shared political aspirations, if not always ideals or principles.

It is worth noting in this connection that before 1789 social and political commentators labored under a double handicap in seeking to analyze the realitities confronting them. In the first place, the cherished medieval vision of orders— noblemen, clergymen, burghers, peasants—seemed less and less meaningful, even when applied to Europeans who quite clearly, in a technical sense, did belong to nobility or clergy, bourgeoisie or peasantry. What real use, one might ask, was a category that covered English dukes, French lawyers, and the *glota*, the "barefoot gentry" of Poland, or Italian cardinals, Spanish friars, and poor German schoolmasters in clerical garb? What was the bourgeois brotherhood that united town patricians with the poor cobbler who stared hopefully at their shoes? What good did it do to call "peasants" both the independent *laboureur* on his French farm and the miserable worker on a Bohemian estate?

A second, still more serious trouble with the language of corps and orders was that it did not apply at all to large numbers of people who nonetheless deserved to be taken very seriously. The new Manchester textile manufacturer, the Genevan watch exporter only lately arrived from Basel or Lausanne, the immigrant Dutch wine merchant in Bordeaux were not legally "bourgeois" of their cities, but they most assuredly were businessmen. And what of the growing army of workers not accommodated by the guild system—to what order did they belong?

Let us not oversimplify. If it would be wrong to assume that European society before 1789 was in fact a tightly knit system of orders, it would be just as great an error to suppose that classes, status groups, and parties were as yet completely invisible. Quite the reverse was true, as we realize when we read bitter strictures concerning "the rich"—English nabobs back from India, French tax contractors, German speculators in grains. There was an old awareness to of "the poor" as a polyglot, urban-rural mass, an awareness born of countless seventeenth-century upheavals and of eighteenth-century troubles as recent as E. I. Pugachev's vast rebellion in Russia. If there were emergent classes, there were also eighteenth-century social elements whose honorific status escaped the traditional definition in terms of orders. We need here mention

only the place occupied in most countries by the higher civil service, the major bureaucrats, often humbly born and only moderately wealthy, whose power nevertheless excited both respect and animosity. . . .

Yet the language of orders hung on until the Great Revolution, and in so far as that language expressed the accepted, the respectable way of describing human relationships, it was itself a conditioning factor in the situation. For while Europe's population was not, in fact had never been, neatly subdivided into nobility, clergy, bourgeoisie, peasantry, and certain less general orders, a conventional terminology suggesting that those were the only meaningful rubrics still helped to shape men's reactions to developments. Edmund Burke, like Montesquieu before him, both pleaded for reform and denounced revolution in the name of healthy relations among stable ranks of men. Gaspar Melchor de Jovellanos, gifted and enlightened though he was, saw fit to dramatize Spain's ills in 1787 by composing a poem on the sad decline of the ancient nobility. . . . Even in the early polemical writings of the French Revolution, notably including those of the Abbé Sieyès, we perceive the hold that old terms and categories had maintained on the political imagination of the day. The confused vehemence of the 1780's, the impression of issues badly joined, not only in France but in other countries as well, seems to me to testify to the inadequacy of an inherited conceptual scheme when applied to recalcitrant circumstances.

It was the pitiless test of power imposed upon most of Europe by the revolutionary-Napoleonic crisis that killed the old image of society—not completely nor all at once, to be sure. Vestiges of archaic language and values have survived to the present day, sometimes twisted to more modern polemical uses. . . . In any case, the false symmetry of a single hierarchy of orders never recovered from the shock it received in the quarter century that opened in 1789.

That the Revolution contained elements of class conflict, in its most precise, economic sense, was apparent even before the Estates-General came together at Versailles. The *Affaire Réveillon* of April 1789, for instance, was a bloody riot touched off by the efforts of two wealthy Parisian manufacturers (members of the Third Estate) to impose lower wage scales. It is my own belief that Marxist historians, from Albert Mathiez to Albert Soboul, have sought to make class conflict explain more facets of the French Revolution than it can in fact account for. It would be foolish, however, to deny that the struggle between poor men and those more comfortable runs back and forth through the historical fabric of the period, from the Faubourg Saint-Antoine to German cities on the Rhine, from the streets of Amsterdam to the shimmering water front of Naples.

At the same time, we also encounter intensified party strife, the competition of political groups for power as an end in itself. The succession of such groups in the French assemblies—Feuillants, Girondists, *Montagnards, Hébertistes*— is so familiar that it can easily be underrated as a new chapter in parliamentary history. No less significant, however, was the effect of events in France on other countries, the tendency in one government after another for "anti-" and "pro-French" parties to appear under such conditions as the local situation offered. In England, for example, war fever and the dread of Jacobin excesses combined to discredit Charles James Fox in the 1790's, but not before his collision with

Pitt had given a new sharpness to the struggle between Whigs and Tories.

Gradations of social status, no less than economic and political alignments, were deeply affected by the upheaval. In France, and in other lands that experienced even a forced transplantation of the Revolution, a decadelong assault both on ecclesiastical independence and on the privileges of birth left the honorific position of clergy and nobility—not to mention their physical base of power, especially in land—damaged beyond hope of complete repair. Admittedly, neither order was destroyed, but henceforth neither could look down with secure disdain on the rest of society. The revolutionaires' glorification of "citizen" as the proudest of all titles, like their insistence that love of country outweighed humble birth, struck at the very roots of inherited rank and at the mystical awe surrounding prelates.

In place of the old determinants of status, certain others gained a degree of general acceptance that they have commanded ever since. I refer to wealth, special abilities, and service to the community (especially if recognized by the bestowal of public office or military rank). Questions might still be asked about an individual's family tree and his way of life, but they seemed less and less relevant when compared with other, more urgent queries: Is he rich or poor? What can he do? What is his present position? The modern status system may seem no more attractive than that of the *ancien régime,* but the differences between the two are unmistakable.

The Imperial Nobility established by Napoleon in 1808 provides somewhat surprisingly, an excellent example of basic change. To a superficial observer it might appear that the Emperor was simply resurrecting aristocratic privilege, as underpinning for his dynasty. But let us not overlook two features of this new hierarchy. First, its titles were assigned on the basis of military services rendered or public offices already held by the recipients. . . . Second, such a title . . . could pass to his descendants only if accompanied by a fortune sufficient to support it. To meet this requirement, a prince of the Empire would have to bequeath an estate yielding at least 200,000 francs per year, while the corresponding figure for a count was 30,000, for a baron 15,000, and for a chevalier 3,000. Napoleon visualized not only a nobility of service, but also one that would remain an "upper class" in specifically economic terms. In his shrewd, cynical mind and in the minds of many of his contemporaries there remained no room for arguments about the virtues of aristocratic birth or leisured refinement or genteel poverty.

I have asked for due consideration of a series of institutional, military, political, and aesthetic changes and, in slightly more detail, a set of complex but crucial changes in social structure. Any one of these factors might in itself be dismissed as unrepresentative, or at most a matter only of degree. Taken together, however, they reveal a revolution in the fullest sense, a fundamental departure from some of the most important conditions of human life before 1789. The magnitude and the nature of this phenonmenon will surely escape the historian whose gaze is riveted on just one country or on only one type of evidence, be it diplomatic correspondence, official enact-

ments, personal reminiscences, or belles-lettres. But the historian who is willing to look up, however briefly, from his specialized labors and to indulge in a panoramic view can scarcely avoid the impression of looking back toward . . . a true watershed.

To recognize such a divide is not to ignore all the important threads of continuity mentioned at this essay's beginning. I do not, for example, support the claim that the men of the old regime are more remote from us than St. Thomas Aquinas was from them. On the other hand, there is little to be gained and much to be lost by overlooking the watershed of the Revolution or by underestimating the effort required for us to think our way back across it into the eighteenth century. In 1789, after long, confused preliminaries, the old Europe began a transformation, convulsive, bewildering, to some of the participants wildly exhilarating, to others bitterly tragic. In 1914 another convulsion began. Its successive spasms were destined to last even longer than those of its predecessor. Its human cost was far more terrible, and it contained much less that was either generous or hopeful. Perhaps the greatest tribute that can now be paid to European civilization, to its vitality, its adaptability, and its tenacity, lies in the observation that through two such cataclysms we can still trace so many familiar lines, truly uniting the centuries. Fully aware of those lines, historians should not shrink from marking the changes along the way.

Suggestions for Further Reading

There exists an enormous literature on the French Revolution. The books listed below must of necessity form a highly selective bibliography designed to give students basic reading on significant aspects of the period. Many of these books contain bibliographic information for further detailed study.

Georges Lefebvre, *La Révolution française* (Paris, 1954) ranks as one of the best general studies of the Revolution; It has recently been published in English in a two-volume edition. Other useful general studies include Crane Brinton, *A Decade of Revolution* (New York, 1935); J.M. Thompson, *The French Revolution* (New York, 1943); Albert Mathiez, *The French Revolution* (New York, 1964; original, 1922–1927); Alfred Goodwin, *The French Revolution* (New York, 1962; original, 1953); Albert Soboul, *La Révolution française*, 2 vols. (Paris, 1964), and Alfred Cobban, *The Social Interpretation of the French Revolution* (London, 1964).

In dealing with the origins of the Revolution, C. E. Labrousse, *La Crise de l'économie française a la fin de l'Ancien Régime et au début de la Révolution* (Paris, 1944) provides a detailed study of the economic circumstances leading to the events of 1789. Mark Block, *French Rural History* (Berkeley, Calif., 1966; original, 1931) describes the outstanding characteristics of prerevolutionary agriculture. Among the more important older treatments of French society is Alexis de Tocqueville, *The Old Regime and the French Revolution* (New York, 1955; original, 1856). More recent studies include Franklin Ford, *Robe and Sword; The Regrouping of the French Aristocracy after Louis XIV* (New York,

1953); Robert Forster, "The Provincial Noble, a Reappraisal," *American Historical Review,* LXVIII (1963), 681–691, and E. Barber, *The Bourgeoisie in 18th Century France* (Princeton, N.J., 1955). For studies of the international background of the revolution, consult Robert R. Palmer, *Age of the Democratic Revolution,* vol. 1 (Princeton, N.J., 1959) and Jacques Godechot, *France and the Atlantic Revolution of the Eighteenth Century, 1770–1799* (New York, 1965).

Georges Lefebvre, *The Coming of the French Revolution* (New York, 1939) ranks among the best studies of the opening years of the revolutionary era. Beatrice Hyslop, *A Guide to the General Cahiers of 1789* (New York, 1968; original, 1936) provides a useful summary of a people's hopes and desires at the outbreak of the Revolution. Jacques Godechot, *Les Institutions de la France sous la Révolution et l'Empire* (Paris, 1951) provides an excellent summary of important legislation during the period. E. Thompson, *Popular Sovereignty and the French Constituent Assembly, 1789–1791* (New York, 1952) describes the major political issues during the first years of the Revolution. Studies of early revolutionary leaders include O. Welch, *Mirabeau* (London, 1951); Louis Gottschalk, *Lafayette,* 4 vols. (Chicago, 1935–1950); and E. Ellery, *Brissot de Warville* (Boston, 1915).

A. Mathiez, *Le Dix août* (Paris, 1931) examines the overthrow of the monarchy; Robert R. Palmer, *Twelve Who Ruled* (New York, 1965; original, 1941) presents a fascinating account of the ensuing crisis and the Reign of Terror. Donald Greer has written two important statistical studies: *The Incidence of*

Emigration during the French Revolution (Cambridge, Mass., 1951) and *The Incidence of the Terror during the French Revolution* (Cambridge, Mass., 1935). Albert Latreille, *L'Eglise Catholique et la Révolution* (Paris, 1946) discusses church-state relations during the entire period. Jacques Godechot. *La Contre-révolution* (Paris, 1961) deals with resistance to the Revolution from 1789 to 1799.

Studies of the Terror and biographies of leading figures during the period 1793–1794 include Crane Brinton, *The Jacobins* (New York, 1968; original, 1930); Michael J. Sydenham, *The Girondins* (London, 1968); J. M. Thompson, *Robespierre*, 2 vols. (London, 1935); A. Mathiez, *Etudes sur Robespierre* (Paris, 1958); L. Gottschalk, *Jean-Paul Marat* (Chicago, 1967; original, 1927); E. Curtis, *Saint-Just* (New York, 1935); Marcel Reinhard, *Le Grand Carnot*, 2 vols. (Paris, 1950–1952); Leo Gershoy, *Bertrand Barere* (Princeton, N.J., 1962); G. Bruun, "The Evolution of a Terrorist; Georges Auguste Couthon," in *Journal of Modern History,* II (1930), 410–429; J. B. Sirich, *The Revolutionary Committees in the Departments of France* (Cambridge, Mass., 1935); and R. B. Rose, *The Enrangés* (Melbourne, Australia, 1965).

Among the works on the popular movement are George Rudé, *The Crowd in the French Revolution* (Oxford, Eng. 1959); Albert Soboul, *Les Sans-Culottes parisiens en l'an*, vol. II (Paris, 1958); and Richard Cobb, *Les Armées révolutionnaires; Instrument de la Terreur dans les départments,* 2 vols. (Paris, 1961–1963). For a critical summary of research on the popular movement see Robert R. Palmer, "Popular Democracy in the French Revolution," in *French Historical Studies,* I (1960), 445–469. Charles Tilly, *The Vendée* (Cambridge, Mass., 1964) discusses the complexities of the counterrevolutionary movement. The Thermidorian reaction and the Directory are described in Georges Lefebvre, *The Thermidorians* (New York, 1966; original, 1937) and his book, *The Directory* (New York, 1966; original, 1946). Other useful works on the Directory include A. Goodwin, "The French Executive Directory — A Revaluation," in

History, XXII (1937), 201–218; G. Homan, "Jean Francois Reubell, Director," in *French Historical Studies,* I (1960), 416–435; G. Robinson, *Revellier Lepeaux* (New York, 1938); and D. Thomson, *The Babeuf Plot* (London, 1947). Jacques Godechot, *Les Commissaires aux armées sous le Directoire,* 2 vols. (Pairs, 1938) presents an interesting and useful summary of civil and military relations from 1795 to 1799.

For a general study of the economic situation during the revolution see A. Chabert, *Essai sur les mouvements des revenus et de l'activité économique en France de 1789 à 1820* (Paris, 1920); S. Clough, *France, A History of National Economics, 1789–1939* (New York, 1939); and F. L. Nussbaum, *Commerical Policy in the French Revolution* (New York, 1923). S. Harris, *The Assignats* (Cambridge, Mass., 1930) is a first-rate study of the French experiments with paper money. Lefebvre *Etudes sur la Révolution française* (Paris, 1963) contains several excellent articles on social and economic problems. Octave Festy, *L'agriculture pendant la Révolution française* (Paris, 1947) contains a good survey of agricultural economics during the revolution, and Georges Dejoint, *La politique économique du Directoire* (Paris, 1951) provides valuable information on the economic situation after 1794.

A general survey of European diplomacy is to be found in A. Sorel, *L'Europe et la Révolution française,* 8 vols. (Paris, 1889–1910). Although somewhat dated, it is still very useful. More recent surveys include E. Bourgeois, *Manuel historique de politique étrangère,* vol. II, *les revolutions* (Paris, 1913), and Raymond Fugier, *La Révolution française et l'Empire Napoleonien,* vol. IV of *Histoire des relations internationales,"* edited by P. Renouvin (Paris, 1954). For works concerning international aspects of the revolution see Jacques Godechot, *La Grande Nation,* 2 vols. (Paris, 1956) and Robert R. Palmer, *The Age of the Democratic Revolution,* vol. II (Princeton, N.J., 1964). Other useful diplomatic studies include S. Biro, *The German Policy of Revolutionary France,* 2 vols. (Cambridge, Mass., 1957); J. H. Clapham, *The Causes of the*

War of 1792 (London, 1899); and Raymond Guyot, *Le Directoire et la paix de l'Europe* (Paris, 1912).

Studies on military affairs include S. Wilkinson, *The French Army before Napoleon* (London, 1930); R. S. Quimby, *The Background of Napoleonic Warfare* (New York, 1957); A. Chuquet, *Les Guerres de la Révolution,* 11 vols. (Paris, 1886–1896); M. Lauerma, *L'Artillerie de campagne française pendant les guerres de la Révolution* (Helsinki, 1957); and Albert Soboul, *Les Soldats de l'an II* (Paris, 1959). Georges Six, *Dictionnaire biographique des géneraux et admiraux français de la Révolution et de l'Empire,* 2 vols. (Paris, 1934) supplies valuable biographical information on French military leaders. His second work *Les géneraux de la Révolution et de l'Empire* (Paris, 1947) studies the generals as a social group. These works deal with the tactics and organization of the French revolutionary armies as well as describing specific battles. For naval affairs see A. T. Mahan's old but still useful *The Influence of Seapower upon the French Revolution and Empire, 1793–1812,* 2 vols. (Boston, 1892); N. Hampson, *La Marine de l'an II* (Paris, 1959); and L. Levy Schneider's biography, *Le Conventionnel Jeanbon Saint-André,* 2 vols. (Paris, 1901). Saint-André was the Committee of Public Safety's naval expert.

On the question of the overall impact of the revolution, F. Ford, "The Revolutionary-Napoleonic Era; How much of a Watershed?" in *American Historical Review,* LXIX (1963) 18–29, summarizes the most recent views on this problem, as does Robert R. Palmer "Recent Interpretation of the Influence of the French Revolution," in *Journal of World History, II* (1954) 173–195.